Healing His Bride

Myhosi "Josie" Ashton, LMHC

FIRST EDITION

ISBN: 979-8-234-04319-1

WHAT OTHERS ARE SAYING

"Everyone is intrigued by celebrities, but the REAL HEROES are standing next to me."

— SALMA HAYEK on marching alongside Josie Ashton, *Marie Claire*, 2002

"I had the privilege of working with Josie Ashton while serving as a Domestic Violence Detective with the Miami Police Department from 1999 to 2001. Even then, Josie demonstrated extraordinary compassion and dedication to helping victims during some of the most difficult moments of their lives. Her voice, insight, and resilience continue to inspire, and this work reflects the same commitment to healing and advocacy that I witnessed firsthand."

— MANUEL A. "MANNY" MORALES Chief of Police, City of Miami Police Department

"When I met Josie Ashton several decades ago, it was when I led a national domestic violence organization and she had started The Brides' March to honor Gladys Ricart. It was an incredible project that grew to become an international event. Her story will lift you and help you find a way to feed your own soul while doing good in the world."

— RITA SMITH, International Expert, Violence Against Women

"With her Dominican roots and her American voice, author Josie Ashton traces the footsteps of a bride killed on her wedding day – a journey of many years she cannot abandon until she finally understands why the story captured her own heart. If you care about women, and tradition, and violence, do not miss this riveting memoir."

— JOHANNA NEUMAN, historian and author of
Gilded Suffragists, And Yet they Persisted, The Concert, and more

"*[Healing His Bride]* offers a powerful reflection on trauma, advocacy, and the often-overlooked emotional toll carried by those who fight for survivors of violence. Josie's journey reminds us that activism alone cannot heal trauma; true transformation requires the bravery to confront our own pain."

— IVON MESA, author of *Why Are We Not Outraged?*

"A courageous and deeply moving testament to the power of truth, faith, and healing. Josie Ashton takes readers on an unforgettable journey from advocacy to self-discovery, reminding us that even those who help heal the world must eventually tend to their own wounds."

— MARK CHRISTOPHER LAWRENCE, two-time Emmy-nominated
actor and comedian

"Twenty-five years later, she has bottled up the essence of this international movement – to end the victim blaming, shame, and self-betrayal that uphold domestic violence – in a memoir. Josie's empathy, clarity of purpose, and brave vulnerability have helped define me and the many others whose lives she has personally touched. I hope you too are transformed through the wisdom of her testimony in this book."

— LETHY DENISE LIRIANO, niece of Gladys Ricart and Executive
Director of National Bride's March

For Adrian Ashton,
who met me with love, believed in my dreams,
and walked beside me without counting the cost.

For Mom and Dad,
I love you, and I thank you for life.

For my daughters—
Stephanie, Savannah, and Sophia—
whose love restored my heart and gave my life
deeper meaning.

For the Ricart Family,
whose courage transformed grief into
a movement of healing.

For Marie-Ann & Lethy Liriano,
thank you for loving and trusting me.

For Jennifer Kent,
His grace is sufficient.
Much love!

And for God,
who lifted me from the miry clay
and renews my mind each day.

Table of Contents

INTRODUCTION

"The beauty of life is captured by simply living
it, in the present, and without judgment."

September 26th, 1999. The date carved itself into my memory like a blade against soft wood – sharp, permanent, unavoidable.

The evening news flickered to life on my television. Adrian sat beside me on our Miami couch, his attention on the national broadcast while I surfed local channels. But that night, every station – English and Spanish – carried the same story. A bride, murdered. On her wedding day. By a jealous ex-boyfriend who couldn't accept her no.

The camera lingered on a wooden floor, on white fabric stained dark. Children being carried from the scene, their faces smeared with tears and disbelief. The news anchor's voice remained steady as he detailed what had happened in Ridgefield, New Jersey, just hours before: Gladys Ricart, dressed in her wedding gown, had been shot five times in her home while her fiancé waited for her at the altar.

I changed the channel. Univision covered it. Telemundo, the same. I could smell the gunpowder through the screen, taste the heat of those bullets. My hands found the remote and clicked the television off. The sudden silence was worse than the noise – too loud, too accusing, too full.

Adrian looked at me, confused. I stood without explanation.

My family watched as I paced our small apartment, back and forth, the carpet wearing thin under my feet. Something was breaking open inside me, something I'd kept carefully sealed. I could feel their eyes following me, puzzled, as this frantic energy overtook my Sunday evening.

I had to move. Had to run. Had to scream. But the words wouldn't come.

The grief arrived like a wave of emotions I didn't understand – raw, unbearable, leaving me gasping. I was paralyzed at the edge of my own reality. I didn't know Gladys Ricart. I had never met her, never heard her name before that night. Yet in that moment, the density of her absence settled on my shoulders like wet sand. I felt trapped, drowning in the aftermath of a tragedy that didn't belong to me. A tragedy I had only witnessed through a flickering screen.

My work in criminal justice had exposed me to crime scenes. I'd seen blood-soaked mattresses at murder scenes, walked the cold corridors of hospital morgues, spent years navigating the wreckage of other people's lives. The work had hardened me, or so I thought.

But Gladys – her murder was something else entirely. A force that shoved me down to a place of despair and grief I'd never accessed before.

Millions witnessed the devastation of this family. Millions saw Gladys's murder from the comfort of their homes as if watching a trailer for an upcoming horror film. Most of us felt the same nauseated disgust, the same cold dread. It wasn't just the violence; it was the deep recognition of friends and families who would suffer for decades to come.

For me, it ripped open wounds I didn't know I had.

My breath became shallow. Memories surfaced – not images exactly, but sensations. The taste of acetic acid in my mouth. The smell of burnt metal. Heat and sweat. All my sensors activated at once.

I was twenty-seven years old. Married. Two daughters. A demanding job. I'd been running on autopilot for years, burying the past under a mountain of responsibilities. Anxiety had become my default setting – work harder, faster, better. Depression hid behind aggression and irritability. But I'd never connected the dots, never dared to dig out the buried pain.

That night, the weight of it all crashed down on me and my family. The fragile home I'd envisioned building was made of breakable glass, and the day Gladys was killed, I started noticing the cracks.

My future – once solid, full of goals with defined objectives and action steps – became a blurry canvas. All of a sudden, I was left with memories to decipher and the aftertaste of past mistakes. The past walked in unannounced and uninvited.

This book is more than words on a page, it is the blueprint I painstakingly drew, tracing the emotional wounds left by storms I didn't choose. For decades I avoided seeing the destruction or assessing the emotional damage. The thought, "I have to rebuild, strengthen, reinforce the fractured foundation" never crossed my mind. Even recently, I've found myself assessing the impact trauma left on the structure of my life. But now a loud voice inside me – my beautiful true voice – reminds me, "You are the architect of your life." Although I did not cause the destruction, it is definitely my job to rebuild.

For those who share the painful silence of trauma, let my testimony offer you hope and inspiration to rebuild your life and design your healing journey. For those who love someone struggling with this complex darkness, this book offers a glimpse into the web of their pain.

This is not a clinical manual. But perhaps you'll find yourself in some of my stories. Each chapter is a step toward finding the wounds in your own narrative. Each sentence can become a melody in the symphony you're preparing to write.

Today, I choose life. I am creating my present and helping design the future I deserve – intentionally, gracefully, patiently.

May my healing journey bring you the necessary peace and hope to contemplate your own.

ONE

I Knew Her

Transformational experiences don't always send the RSVP, sometimes it simply arrives during a normal Sunday evening. The screen glowed in the dim living room. My fingers already surfing through the local stations. Channel 7. Channel 10. Back to 4.

It was the repetition that caught my attention first. The same footage on every channel, the same desperate quality in the reporters' voices. My thumb hovered over the remote.

A house in New Jersey. Police tape. A crowd of people in formal clothes, their faces twisted in grief. The camera zoomed tighter: a woman in a wedding gown being placed into a coroner's van instead of the Rolls Royce waiting for her outside of her house.

The news anchor's voice sharpened, grew more detailed: "Thirty-nine-year-old Gladys Ricart was shot five times in her Ridgefield home early this evening. The suspect, identified as her ex-boyfriend Agustin Garcia, walked in the house and opened fire as Ricart prepared to leave for her wedding ceremony. Her fiancé,

James Preston, was waiting at the Church on the Hill in Flushing, New York."

My chest tightened while my stomach revolted.

The screen cut to footage of a church. I could imagine the guests standing outside, confusion turning to alarm, cell phones pressed to ears. The reporter continued: "Several family members were present, including Ricart's twenty-year-old son. Multiple witnesses have been taken to police headquarters for questioning."

"My goodness," Adrian breathed beside me.

I clicked to Univision. The same images, but now the reporter spoke rapid Spanish — *novia, asesinada, novio esperando en la iglesia.* The words felt closer somehow, more intimate. My grandmother's language. My mother's language. The language of my childhood.

I switched again. Telemundo. CNN Español. Every channel showed that house in Ridgefield, that white dress, that unthinkable violence.

My fingers moved without conscious thought, turning off the television. The sudden silence filled the room like only death can.

"Josie?" Adrian's hand touched my shoulder.

I stood. My legs carried me to the window, then back to the couch, then to the doorway. I could feel my daughters watching from their bedroom door — Stephanie, eight years old, holding Savannah's hand. I could feel my abuela's concerned gaze from her chair in the corner.

"*Mija,*" Abuela started.

"I'm fine," I heard myself say. But I wasn't fine. My heart pounded against my ribs. Heat crawled up my neck and face. The living room felt too small, the walls pressing in.

I paced. Kitchen to living room. Living room to hallway. Back again.

"Maybe you should sit down," Adrian suggested, his lawyer's voice careful and measured.

I shook my head. If I sat, if I stopped moving, something inside me would break open. I could feel it there, just beneath the surface – something massive and terrifying that had been waiting for years to emerge.

"Did you know her?" Adrian asked. "From work, maybe?"

"No." The word came out strangled. "I've never heard of her."

But that wasn't entirely true. I hadn't heard her *name* before. But I knew her. Somehow, impossibly, I knew her. I knew what it felt like to wear a wedding dress and feel your life about to change. I knew what it meant to be a Dominican woman building a future in America. I knew what it was like to love someone, to plan for forever, to believe you were finally safe.

And I knew – God help me, I knew intimately – what it meant to run from a man who couldn't accept your no.

The memories came flooding: Mike's hands around my throat in that Miami International Airport. My mother's face after her boyfriend's beatings. The neighbor who cornered me when I was nine. The family members whose touches lingered too long, their laughter when I tried to pull away.

My breath shortened. In through the nose, out through the mouth. The coping techniques I'd taught countless victims suddenly useless in my own body.

"*Josie, siéntate.*" Abuela's voice, firmer now. "*Estás asustando a las niñas.*" I'm scaring the girls.

I looked at Stephanie and Savannah. Their eyes were wide, uncertain. They'd never seen me like this – their mother who walked through courtrooms with confidence, who advocated for victims without flinching, who held crying strangers and promised them justice.

"Sorry," I managed. "I'm sorry. I just need – I need some air."

I walked out to our small balcony. The Miami night was thick and humid, but I gulped it in anyway. Below, the parking lot stretched out under yellow streetlights. Cars passed on the main road. Normal life continuing while somewhere in New Jersey, a bride was dead and a family's world as they knew it had painfully disintegrated.

I gripped the railing until my knuckles turned white.

Gladys Ricart. I repeated her name in my mind, committing it to memory. Gladys Ricart was supposed to get married today. Gladys Ricart had a son. Gladys Ricart said no to a man, and that man killed her for it.

The sliding door opened behind me. Adrian stepped out, his presence solid and warm.

"Talk to me," he said quietly.

"I can't." My voice cracked. "I don't even understand it myself."

He moved beside me, his shoulder touching mine. We stood in silence, the sounds of our neighborhood drifting up – a dog barking, a car door slamming, someone's television through an open window.

"It's not just her, is it?" Adrian finally asked. "It's bringing something else up."

I nodded, not trusting my voice.

"Okay." He squeezed my hand. "Okay. We'll figure it out."

But I wasn't sure we would. Because something had shifted in me that night, something foundational. The careful compartments I'd built – childhood trauma here, teenage abuse there, adult success; keeping it all separate – had begun to collapse. And Gladys Ricart, a woman I'd never met, had become the earthquake that brought it all down.

Inside, I could hear Abuela getting the girls ready for bed. The familiar sounds of our evening routine. But I couldn't move yet. I stayed on that balcony, my eyes fixed on nothing, my mind spinning with images of white dresses and broken promises and women who dared to say no.

I stayed there until the streetlights blurred with my tears, until Adrian's arm around my shoulders was the only thing keeping me upright, until I understood with cold certainty that my life had just divided into before and after this moment.

Before I knew Gladys's name.

After I could never unknow it.

The next morning, I called Adrian's mother. My hands shook as I dialed.

"Hey Moma Josie, I was hoping you'd call," Doreen answered, her voice heavy. "Did you see it?"

"I saw it."

"That poor soul. That poor family." A pause. "Are you okay?"

I heard the question which remained floating in the air until I caught a hold of it. Was I okay? I was functioning. I'd gotten the girls ready for school, made breakfast, put on my work clothes. From the outside, I looked okay.

"I don't know," I admitted. "Moma Doreen, I can't stop thinking about her."

"I know, Josie. I know."

"Can you–" I swallowed hard. "Can you send me the news articles? The New York papers must be covering it."

"Of course." Her voice was gentle, understanding without needing explanation. "I'll mail them to you today."

I went to work. Sat at my desk at the Miami-Dade State Attorney's Office. Answered phones, processed paperwork, reviewed victim impact statements. But my mind kept returning to that house in Ridgefield. To a bride who never made it to her own wedding. To a man who'd rather kill her than let her go.

And underneath it all, like a drumbeat I couldn't silence: *This matters. This changes everything. Pay attention.*

That Sunday night in September, I only knew that something inside me had cracked wide open, and there would be no going back.

TWO
His Plan

The domestic violence conference room in Destin, Florida hummed with the familiar energy of advocates sharing their stories. October 2000. I should have been taking notes nodding along with presentations on crisis intervention and trauma-informed care. Most of that day I had done all the right things. But now, instead, I was drowning.

The young woman on stage had survived something unspeakable. She sat in a wheelchair, her voice steady despite the tremor in her hands as she described the violence that had shattered her spine. Around me, seasoned professionals leaned forward, scribbling notes. I felt my throat starting to close.

I mumbled something to my four colleagues who had joined me – an excuse, an apology – and stumbled toward the exit. Jasmine's concerned face blurred in my peripheral vision as I pushed through the doors into the humid October night.

The villa's air conditioning hit me like a wall of ice. I fumbled with the lock, my hands shaking so badly I nearly dropped the key. The floorboards creaked under the weight of my footsteps, each step echoing my internal turmoil. Inside, I collapsed against the door, my breath coming in ragged gasps.

What is wrong with you? The familiar voice of self-recrimination started its litany. *You work with victims every day. You've seen worse. You've processed crime scene photos, held mothers as they identified their children's bodies. Why is this different?*

But I knew why. Gladys's face – the photograph that had consumed me for a year now – floated before my eyes. The wedding dress. The blood. The camera crews turning tragedy into spectacle.

I collapsed beside the bed, still wearing my conference badge and heels. My face was buried in the mattress. The tears came then, a torrent of anguish. I didn't understand why I cried, only that it was bigger than me, something beyond my comprehension, something… sacred.

My knees pressed into the plush carpet. I squeezed my eyes shut, as if that could somehow block out the overwhelming feeling.

Then something shifted.

The air grew thick, almost viscous. Not the humidity – something else. Something that made the hair on my arms stand up, made my skin prickle with sudden heat despite the aggressive AC.

I sat up slowly, my heart hammering. The room looked the same. Nothing had moved. But the presence was undeniable – a pressure, a fullness, as if the space itself had inhaled and was now holding its breath.

"Hello?" My voice came out as a whisper.

The silence pressed down. Not empty silence, but loaded, expectant. Like standing in a cathedral at midnight, alone but not alone.

My Christian upbringing surged back – Mama's lessons about being still and knowing, about making space for the holy. But I'd been running from that part of myself for years, burying it under busy-ness and achievement and the desperate need to prove my worth through work.

"I'm not ready," I said aloud, then immediately felt foolish. Ready for what?

The presence intensified. I felt it in my chest, a warmth radiating outward from my entire body. My breathing slowed without my conscious effort. The panic attack that had been building up released its grip.

I closed my eyes.

Immediately, colors exploded behind my eyelids – orange and red, swirling like autumn leaves caught in a whirlwind. The leaves moved with purpose, forming a pattern, a path. I saw myself walking, but not on a street. On a long highway, cars passing, the sun beating down.

And I was wearing white.

My wedding dress.

The image crystallized with devastating clarity, as clear as the news report of September 26, 1999.

I was not just wearing the dress, but walking in it. What kind of walk was this? A processional? A pilgrimage? A funeral? I had so many questions, but I was afraid to ask.

Mile after mile. People stopping their cars, rolling down windows, asking questions. My feet hurting. My legs aching. The dress growing dirty with road dust.

The swirling colors slowed, settled. Now I saw faces – women's faces, mostly. Some crying. Some angry. Some holding children. They stood along the route, watching me pass. Bearing witness.

Then a voice. Not audible, but clear as thunder:

Walk in your wedding dress, and change the headlines about Gladys Ricart.

I gasped, my eyes flying open. The room spun. I gripped the bedspread, wetting the fabric with my sweaty palms.

"Walk where?" I asked the empty room. "Change them how?"

But even as I asked, I knew. New Jersey to Miami. The crime scene where Gladys died to the city where I also wore a wedding gown to marry twice before but survived. Over a thousand miles. In my wedding gown. Telling her story. Changing the narrative from "crime of passion" to murder. From Manslaughter to First Degree Murder. From judging and shaming to educating and restoring.

"That's insane," I said firmly. "I have two children. A husband. A job. I tried to run a 5K last year and nearly died. I can't–"

The presence didn't argue. It simply waited.

I stood on shaking legs and walked to the bathroom, splashed cold water on my face. In the mirror, my reflection looked wild –

mascara smudged, eyes too bright, hair escaping its careful conference-appropriate bun.

"Adrian will think I've lost my mind," I told my reflection.

But even as I said it, I believed that wasn't true. Adrian, who'd grown up in New York, who'd seen the coverage of Gladys's murder, who understood the legal implications of calling it a "crime of passion" – he would understand. Or at least, he would try.

I returned to the bedroom and sat on the edge of the bed, more composed now. The presence remained, patient and implacable.

"If this is You," I said carefully, not sure who I was addressing but needing to say it anyway, "if this is really from You, then You're going to have to open every door. I'm not begging. I'm not convincing anyone. If You want me to do this, You make it happen."

The audacity of my words shocked me even as they left my mouth. Who was I to make demands of God? But I was also done pretending to be someone I wasn't. Done with the performance of false humility. If this vision was divine, then the divine could handle my honesty.

The presence seemed to shift – not withdrawing, but... amused? As if my defiance was expected, even welcomed.

I lay back on the bed, exhausted. The vision remained clear in my mind, but the overwhelming pressure had eased. I felt simultaneously terrified and strangely peaceful.

Through the thin walls, I heard laughter – other conference attendees returning from the evening reception. Normal people having normal conversations about normal professional challenges, while I'm lost in a vision I can barely comprehend.

I thought about Jasmine who had been my rock at work, probably worried about me. About the workshops I'd miss if I couldn't pull myself together. About the woman in the wheelchair whose story had triggered this entire cascade.

But mostly I thought about Gladys.

I'd never met her. Never would. But for the past year, she'd followed me. Every news article I'd collected, every anniversary marked, every time I saw a bride – Gladys was there. Not as a stalker, but as a call. An invitation.

Walk.

The word echoed in my mind, simple and devastating.

I rolled onto my side, pulling my knees toward my chest. The bedspread smelled like industrial detergent and sea salt. Outside, palm fronds scratched against the window in the ocean breeze.

"Okay," I whispered finally. "If You open the doors, I'll walk."

The presence lingered a moment longer, then receded like a tide going out. The room returned to normal, nothing special. But I was changed.

I thought about my life, which had been complex during childhood until my late teens, but now almost picture-perfect. I had been a homeowner at 22, embarking on my career in criminal justice. Although my first marriage ended in divorce at 24, I had a beautiful daughter, Stephanie. My second marriage was to a wonderful man named Adrian – a lawyer I adored – who was now waiting at home with our daughter Savannah. We'd talked excitedly about a new, bigger house to match our growing family. Our beautiful Miami

Lakes apartment, the girls thriving in their excellent schools… it all seemed idyllic.

I thought about the conversation we'd now need to have. About how to explain a divine mandate to a man who loved me, but whose faith was much stronger than I thought.

I thought about my job – I was a star performer at work, the awards and commendations lining my office walls were a testament to my dedication. My colleagues, even in that fiercely competitive '90s environment for women, respected me, admired me. I had friends, laughter… a full, rich life. Would they understand?

I thought about my body – soft, untrained, carrying extra weight from two pregnancies and too many years behind a desk. Could I even walk twenty miles in a day? Could I sustain that for weeks?

But mostly I thought about Gladys. About the photos I'd collected of her smiling with her son, wearing her wedding gown, moments before everything shattered. About the headlines that called it a crime of passion, as if love and murder were synonyms. About her family, devastated, watching the narrative spin away from truth toward spectacle.

Walk in your wedding dress, and change the headlines.

It wasn't just about Gladys anymore. It was about every woman who'd died at the hands of a jealous partner. Every family told their daughter had "provoked" her own murder. Every court system that treated intimate partner violence as a private matter rather than a crime.

The vision had shown me something else too, something I'd barely processed in the moment: I wasn't alone on this highway.

There were others walking with me. Not physically – I'd be alone in the dress. But spiritually, metaphorically, actually: thousands of women and men, bearing witness, joining the procession, refusing to let these deaths be forgotten or minimized.

When I finally drifted into an uneasy sleep, I dreamed of highways stretching endlessly ahead, of a white dress that never got dirty despite the miles, of faces appearing in windows as I passed – surprised, moved, inspired. In the dream, I wasn't tired. My feet didn't hurt. I just kept walking, step after step, mile after mile, toward something I couldn't quite see but knew was necessary.

I awoke the next morning with sunlight streaming through the villa windows, the vision remained clear. Not a dream. Not wishful thinking. A call.

On the flight home, I stared out the window at the landscape far below – roads and highways threading through cities and farmland. Somewhere down there was the route I'd take. New Jersey to Florida. September 26, 2001 to… whenever I finished…

Every mile was an opportunity to perfect my increasingly frantic internal monologue. The image kept playing in my mind: me, in a wedding gown, a vision as sharp and unsettling as a freshly cut diamond.

Panic took over as I entered the apartment. My daughters, Stephanie and Savannah, greeted me with hugs and laughter. Abuela, who moved to the US to help us after my grandfather passed away, was essential in caring for my girls and supporting my work and studies.

Adrian, however, merely watched, his brow furrowed, his usual easy smile absent. His eyes, usually sparkling with affection, held a troubled question. He saw the remnants of tears staining my cheeks. He knew something had happened.

Four years together, two years married. I was certain this vision, this bizarre thing where I put on my wedding gown and walk somewhere for something, would be hard for him to grasp.

That evening, after the girls were asleep, I found Adrian on the bed, his initial curiosity morphing into a worried frown. Tears streamed down my face, blurring his features. "Don't interrupt," I choked out, the words laced with an urgency that surprised even me. He'd never been one to hold back, but this time, his usual interruptions were silenced.

My voice, a torrent of words, blamed his mother first – the articles, those damning articles from Gladys, were her doing, weren't they? A twitch at the corner of his mouth betrayed his amusement; it was a ray of sunshine in the storm of my emotions, and eased the tension in my chest.

I breathed, steadied myself, and my words flowed with a new, surprising eloquence.

"I had a vision," I began, then immediately wanted to stop and judge how ridiculous it sounded. But Adrian just waited, his face open and curious. I told him everything. The presence in the villa. The swirling leaves. The voice. The command. My fears. My anxieties. All of it.

In response, I did not receive an *are you crazy?* There was no *absolutely not.* Just: how would we make it work?

Panic-stricken, I said, "You'll have to stay with the kids while I... I walk," I gasped, the image of my solitary walk unbearable. There was an "Okay," a declaration of accountability, a promise that he would be there, holding me to my impulsive, wildly unconventional plan. And he did.

"And I'll probably lose my job!" The sobs started again, a wrenching, uncontrollable wave. His hug was tight, his murmured "everything will be okay" a fragile raft in a stormy sea, a promise I wasn't entirely sure I believed.

But his reassurances, his promises of unwavering support kept me together.

A lot was planned, a lot discussed, but it boiled down to one step at a time: Tomorrow I'd return to the office. Tomorrow I'd start researching how to contact a grieving family in New Jersey. Tomorrow I'd begin the impossible process of turning a vision into reality.

To me, all that mattered, was that I sat with my husband, listening to the sounds of our daughters sleeping, and felt the strange peace of a decision made.

The walk hadn't begun yet. But in that moment, in that conversation, in that willingness to trust what I'd experienced – it had already started.

God had spoken. I had said yes.

Now I just had to figure out how to actually do it.

THREE
Planted In Mud

The white patent leather shoes, delicate white ruffle socks, and sky-blue dress lay on the bed. I kept moving as Abuela tried to curl my hair. "Sit still," she reminded me, pulling each curl with a firm grip. "Ouch," I'd say, longing for her to finish and imagining the party that awaited.

My busy toes were tapping to the rhythm of my joyful heart which pounded with excitement – the day had finally arrived. The gentle curls, the violet cologne, everything was perfect, meticulously planned. I was ready to twirl at one of the greatest celebrations of life: my cousin's wedding.

I looked stunning. I walked into the living room to model my perfect style for my grandfather, Abuelo.

"Te ves hermosa, mi reyna," You look beautiful my queen, he said, smiling with love and reverence.

Every time Abuelo spoke words of affirmation, his face left me wondering – as if he had more to say, but words failed him. I was

21

only eight years old, but even then, I could read every word on his face. I could read his hugs, the way his hand rested on my head, his deep eye contact as he watched me, shaking his head slowly, as if he saw something in me only, he could see. Something powerful. Something royal. I sensed his awe, and in his presence, I felt mighty, like I could do anything.

Without any warning, the rain started beating on the thin metal roof of our wooden house. Every drop created a melody that I simply did not want to hear! I ran to the window, full of anticipation – and that's when it hit me. The mud.

"No, no, wait!" I shouted. "Abuela! The mud is going to dirty my shoes, my socks, my toes, my dress!"

The heat and humidity turned into sweat, and my anxiety only intensified. My face was damp with moisture as my smile gave way to a frown of worry.

I had always loved the rain – but not that day. That day, the rain turned my joy into a cruel joke. The heavy downpour mixed with the dark orange clay of our rural village, creating a thick, sticky mess that threatened everything I had so carefully prepared.

It was more than mud. It was the idea that, as a young girl, attending a wedding made me almost as important as the bride herself. I needed to be impeccable. I needed to be clean. I needed to be perfect. I was to be a future bride – and my cleanliness and demure behavior reflected my worth.

Without a shadow of a doubt, I realized that on that special night, filth was my destiny.

My grandmother's words did not comfort me: "Plastic bags. I will cover your feet with plastic bags, and you must be very careful as we walk toward the main road."

Very careful, I murmured. *I can't be careful. It's not in me to be careful.* Grandma always told me I was careless, sassy, clumsy, and forgetful.

👣

What kept me strong on that muddy walk was the memory of making the wedding cake. It was 1980, in the Dominican Republic. At that time, wedding cakes were often made at the bride's home. I was assigned the task of mixing vanilla, sugar, and butter until the granules dissolved for the sugar frosting decorations. Hand-mixed, for hours, on and on. What began as a fun task quickly became an excruciating chore.

At that young age, I desperately craved the approval of the women around me – a love I understood to be conditional, based entirely on obedience and performance. Helping in the kitchen was just another test, a chance to prove my worth.

To my delight, the sweet aroma of the batter baking to perfection eventually brought comfort. That was how I knew I belonged. I had earned my place in the kitchen by staying in the kitchen. At last, I was worthy.

The sugar roses, adorned with pearls and intricate details, were breathtaking. The towering cake – a three-tiered masterpiece – stood as a symbol of the ceremony's significance. All that work, the dedication, the sleepless nights, the sacrifice – all for one night. Only years later would I realize that those moments in the kitchen were the prelude to a life of hard work. A life where only true commitment, consistency, and love could sustain a marriage.

❦

A *boda*, or wedding, represents the joining of two families. This isn't just a definition – it's a deep-rooted cultural truth. In Dominican tradition, marriage is a sacred ritual, witnessed with reverence by the couple, the community, and society as a whole. It's a feeling I still carry deep in my bones.

We revere the bride – beautiful and radiant in ivory lace – descending from a waiting car, her eyes full of hope, ready for the complicated task ahead.

It is the beauty in our walk, the elegance in our stride, that we carry to the altar. We walk toward a future we think we understand – but sometimes don't. The groom proposes. But it is the bride who takes the necessary steps, and sometimes many more, to secure his love and exchange their vows.

❦

The energy was palpable as we arrived at my cousin's wedding. Every member of my family had a smile on their faces as they danced, shared welcoming hugs, and commented on the gentle beauty of the evening. I remember the dizzying spin of the *guagua*, the bus ride home, my ears still ringing with the celebratory shouts, the taste of wedding cake lingering sweetly on my tongue.

Car horns blared a celebratory fanfare as drivers leaned out their windows, swept up in the contagious joy. It didn't matter whether they knew the happy couple or not – the unfiltered, unrestrained joy was enough. This was the building of a family. The bedrock of community. Visible. Tangible. Real.

Years later, when I saw Gladys Ricart on my television screen – her wedding gown soaked in blood, her family's joy turned to horror – I understood why that image broke something in me that had never fully healed.

A bride killed on her wedding day was the destruction of everything sacred I had learned as that eight-year-old girl walking through mud, desperate to stay clean, desperate to be worthy.

Gladys never got to taste her wedding cake. She never got to hear the car horns celebrating her joy. She never got to walk down that aisle in her perfectly clean dress, her family watching with pride.

Instead, she became a different kind of bride – a symbol of every woman who tried to walk away from violence and was struck down for it. A reminder that sometimes the mud doesn't just dirty our shoes. That sometimes, it swallows us whole.

At a young age, I started to feel like I was drowning in that same mud. The rocking chair on my grandparents' porch was my playground. I used to rock so hard that one day I flipped forward, and the heavy iron chair crashed down on top of me. I remember the relief I felt when I heard a pot slam to the floor in the kitchen. Abuela had heard me crying. She was coming.

Her steps were firm – urgent. I could hear her breathing grow heavier as she got closer. My legs were trapped beneath the cold iron frame, but my fear began to dissolve as I felt her presence near me. Those rocking chairs were built to last generations. That day, it felt like it would last longer than me.

Her wet hands – damp from washing dishes – grabbed my skinny brown arms. My hands were soaked with tears and sweat. Even through blurry eyes, I saw something in her face: determination. She would rescue me. That much was certain.

What I did not expect was what came next.

She had somehow picked up Abuelo's belt on her way to save me.

She pulled the chair off my legs. She rendered aid. And then she inflicted wounds. The belt hurt far more than the iron ever did. In that moment, I almost wished I had stayed pinned beneath the chair.

That was Abuela's discipline – swift, intentional, severe. She never struck blindly. She prepared. She wrapped the belt tightly around her hand, pulled back her torso to gain momentum, and delivered her punishment with precision. The welts would rise warm and swollen on my skin. My heart would pound. My bladder and stomach would tighten. My nervous system would shut down. I wasn't thinking – I was surviving.

I began to notice patterns. What weapon she chose. Where she aimed. How hard she struck depending on the offense. It was research. I watched a woman with the face of an angel transform into someone unrecognizable. I studied her the way a child studies weather – trying to predict storms.

One day in the kitchen, she confronted me about a letter I had written to a neighbor. When I admitted it, she slapped me so hard my head snapped sideways. I was ten years old. That was the day shame introduced itself to me.

I used to beg during the beatings.

"Please, Grandma, please. I won't do it again."

I begged as if I had committed a capital crime. The belt never softened.

Eventually, I stopped pleading. I refused to humiliate myself asking for mercy from someone who was supposed to love me. Instead, I dared her.

"Go ahead. Hit me harder."

When the belts were no longer enough, she used an electric cord. The marks lasted weeks. The shame lasted a lifetime.

Spankings were common in her house – as common as the four iron rocking chairs on the porch. Mistakes, even innocent ones, required correction.

One Saturday morning, she tied me to the kitchen table so I would memorize multiplication tables. The smell of frying onions filled the air while I whispered numbers through trembling lips. She didn't know multiplication tables herself. She could barely read or write. I realize now that my academic struggles probably embarrassed her. Her shame became my punishment.

Abuela had the face of an angel and the hand of a lion.

She was born in the countryside near what is now Punta Cana. My great-grandparents owned cattle and land. Life was survival. You worked. You endured. You didn't discuss feelings.

Her upbringing explains so much.

She moved from the countryside to the city after marrying my grandfather – a man who already had children and later fathered another child outside their marriage. She carried humiliation quietly. She cooked. She cleaned. She stayed.

Her love language was service. Breakfast, lunch, dinner, fruit before bed. We never went without food. But we went without softness.

I wanted her hands to soothe me. Instead, they corrected me.

As I grew older, I began to see her differently. Beneath her rage was fear. Beneath her harshness was shame. She held her hands tightly in her lap as she aged, as if gripping control that always felt like it might slip away.

She loved me fiercely. She simply did not know how to show it without control.

Abuelo was different.

His hugs were healing. His love had no conditions. It wasn't tied to grades or behavior. When he was sober, he was calm, thoughtful, affectionate. He brought fruit home. Sometimes candy just for me. He shared the best piece of meat from his plate. His love never shamed me.

But alcohol was his companion. Daily. Functional, but constant.

His laughter from his small dairy factory in the back of the house grounded me. The smell of cheese, butter, and rum followed him everywhere. He was joyful after a few drinks – singing, greeting strangers, generous. And then the drinking grew heavier. The factory disappeared. A truck accident shattered his leg and whatever stability remained. He lost everything but the bottle.

Abuela stayed.

She washed his clothes. Carried water. Tended to him. Her devotion never wavered, even as resentment settled into her bones. Those were the same hands I longed for to comfort me – hands built for labor, not tenderness.

Our home became a place of tension – explosive arguments, long silences, shame floating in the air. I learned to tiptoe. We muted our laughter. We anticipated storms.

The smallest mistake could ignite her.

As a child, I felt like I carried an emotional backpack filled with burdens that were not mine – her disappointments, her anger, her humiliation. I wasn't trying to be compassionate. I was trying to survive.

Over time, I understood something powerful:

Unhealed shame metastasizes.

It moves through families like wildfire. We covered wounds with fashion, makeup, religion, alcohol, sugar – anything to shift the pain. We mastered functioning in chaos. We learned to walk in daylight as if it were darkness.

For years, I walked without knowing where I was going. I believed if I kept moving, I would eventually arrive somewhere safe.

But movement without identity is dangerous.

You can have opportunity, resources, even success – and still be lost. Winning without healing is empty. Achievement without authenticity is fragile.

Healing before winning is not optional. It is essential.

Because if you do not know who you are, if you have not faced your wounds, you will build a life that looks successful and still feel dead inside.

I learned that the hard way.

And I survived long enough to tell the truth.

FOUR
Mama's Walk

The aroma hit me before I even opened the gate – dark, rich, impossibly smooth. Coffee and Mama were inseparable. People drink coffee, but my father's mother orchestrated an entire ritual around it, a performance of Dominican hospitality that could trap the unwary neighbor for hours.

"Mija, cuélamele un café a la vecina." Her voice would boom from the kitchen before the poor woman had even crossed the threshold. *"Vecina, no se vaya, bébase un chin de café ante de irse."*

Translation: Daughter – which could be any female within earshot – brew some coffee for our neighbor. Neighbor, wait, don't leave yet, drink a little coffee first.

A "little bit" meant four ounces of pure, dark, organically grown perfection, sweetened with four to six teaspoons of brown sugar. White sugar was expensive; brown sugar was what we had. And Mama's generosity with it matched her generosity with everything else – abundant, relentless, impossible to refuse.

The neighbor would search desperately for an escape route: *"Es que tengo una úlcera en el estomago."* I have a stomach ulcer.

Wrong answer.

Mama was a nurse. This medical excuse transformed into a thirty-minute dissertation on the healing properties of *boruga* – curdled milk, our Dominican version of yogurt, also sweetened with generous amounts of brown sugar. The same girl who brewed the coffee would now be dispatched to check the refrigerator while the neighbor, who had been heading toward the door, would resign herself to sitting down for an enormous cup of either the coffee or the *boruga*.

I watched this performance unfold countless times. As a child, I thought Mama was simply being kind. As I grew older, I understood: she was forcing intimacy. Creating connection. Insisting on closeness in a world that often-left people isolated and alone.

I surrendered easily to her love. I surrendered easily to all their love – my paternal family's fierce, unapologetic affection – because I desperately needed it. I lacked love in my primary home. I needed affirmations, attention, encouragement. I needed someone to see me.

Mama saw me.

Every visit began the same way: her massive hand engulfing mine, her voice announcing our presence to the entire neighborhood.

"¡Mi primera nieta!"

My first granddaughter.

She'd beam down at me while I squinted up into the sun, my two ponytails dangling awkwardly as yet another neighbor smiled at the top of my head. Don Rafael, who owned the chicken slaughterhouse across the street, would wave from his doorway. The woman at the corner house would pause her sweeping to hear Mama's introduction. The pharmacist, the corner store owner, every single person we passed – all of them would receive the same proclamation.

"My first granddaughter. Isn't she beautiful?"

I don't remember being embarrassed. I remember feeling important.

The walks were more than strolls. They were declarations. Mama claimed me publicly, repeatedly, defiantly. Because claiming me required defiance.

My maternal grandmother, Abuela – Doña Carmen – didn't always want to let me go for weekend visits with my father's family. The phone arguments were legendary. Mama would call, Abuela would refuse, and Mama would show up anyway.

My heart would leap when I heard the taxi door slam, or when I'd see her massive figure at the iron gate, shouting at our open front door:

"¡Doña Carmen, ábrame el portón que yo vine a recoger a mi nieta que a mí me toca!"

Open the gate, Ms. Carmen. I'm here to pick up my granddaughter. It's my turn.

Her voice didn't stutter. Her defiance was unapologetic. I felt every step of those five kilometers as she carried me home.

Their confrontations reminded me of wrestling matches. No real physical violence, every move carefully choreographed with plenty of hostility, drama, and inevitable victory for Mama. I never missed an episode. She always brought home the championship belt: me.

Whether my father was a hundred miles away or just across town, Mama would do whatever was necessary to bring me into her home for family gatherings. Her presence was soothing amidst the chaos of cousins and uncles, always ensuring I was nestled within that swirling vortex of love.

On our walks, she'd take my hand the way my father used to. I could hear her heavy breathing as we sang old hymns together. We'd burst into laughter when I forgot the words or sang the wrong lyrics completely.

She told me stories, sweet stories that filled my spirit. Stories of love, joy, and hope. Never scary stories. Always beautiful stories.

Sometimes I'd share my own stories. They were sad sometimes. But she always listened, no matter how long I talked. She'd always say something encouraging, her words accentuated by a bright smile that highlighted every wrinkle on her face.

Mama laughed with her entire body. When she laughed, every muscle engaged – her tongue, her face, her massive frame shaking with mirth. The sound was contagious. My heart laughs just thinking about her.

A few of my siblings and cousins inherited her laughter. Mama taught us to laugh with gusto, to savor moments, to appreciate the people who arrived in our lives.

Our walks would be interrupted constantly by neighbors recognizing her, wanting to say hello. She'd wave without stopping, shouting back: *"¡Mi primera nieta!"* And the fanfare would start all over again.

This continued until I was a young teenager. There was always a new neighbor to introduce me to. Those long walks with Mama are some of my most precious childhood memories. A few of my only wholesome memories without trauma or fear attached to them.

Love was her only weapon. Her only sword. Her words were sometimes loud and authoritative but always rooted in love.

Our walks together were symbols of her love for me.

Mama's body – a mountain of flesh with curves developed through decades of childbearing and caring for her children – never stopped her. The health issues and daily chores – none of it mattered.

If she didn't have money for a taxi, a neighbor to drive her, or a relative to pick me up, Mama would walk.

The distance didn't matter. She would simply walk to get me.

Years later, as an adult, the melody of Helen Baylor's "Testimony" – the achingly familiar "Praying Grandmother" – still brings a lump to my throat.

This song, it's Mama's essence.

It captures her steady, loving determination to introduce me to her God. Her hand in mine during church. Her reverence as she listened to the preacher. Her strength and her faith.

A faith that would save my life many times. Protect my family. Allow me to flourish despite the obstacles set before me at such an early age.

Mama must have known how much I would need her spiritual teachings. How much I would need the Word. How much I would need a Savior.

So many times, that faith, the faith she taught me was all I had.

As a young adult, I could tell Mama anything. Her faith was lived through and through. The unwavering kindness in her gaze disarmed me. She didn't judge. She embraced me.

She loved me recklessly, unapologetically, unconditionally.

Mama had ten children, including two sets of twins. One set she lost shortly after birth. One son was born with special needs – my uncle Piko who loved me endlessly, who would wait for my visits and make up songs to sing with my name in it with pure devotion.

She served her family daily. Yet somehow, she still had love to give in abundance to each and every grandchild.

Mama never had to fight to spend time with another grandchild the way she fought for me. As the first granddaughter, I occupied a special place. Sometimes cousins would ask me clarifying questions about family traditions or simmering disputes. Occasionally I'd meet with siblings – always a risky endeavor – and we'd have lovely conversations while trying to piece together fragments of our unshared childhood.

My family dynamics were complex. But so were their unwavering faith, their tireless work ethic, their overflowing generosity.

As I've traveled the unpaved roads of my childhood memories, I've discovered that some family members demand and deserve honor. Others, forgiveness. Others, simply an acknowledgment.

Their faces, once fading in my memory, have become clearer. Their deeds, sharper.

I wish I'd learned at a young age how to navigate the rough waters of family history. I wish the emotional fractures had been addressed earlier. I wish the family had found a voice of reason, a voice of unity, a voice of love.

We lost that voice when we lost Mama.

Mama died June 19th, 2004, a mere week before my 32nd birthday. Our last conversation left me speechless while also placing a burden on me that will cost me a lot to carry but I could not refuse. Mama was worried, her soul was not at peace during our last telephone conversation. Her pain from her long battle with cancer was not what she wanted to convey to me in our last conversation. Her main concern was about one of my cousins, who had relocated to Santo Domingo.

Grandma was worried. She did not like the living arrangements, and she was worried about my cousin's wellbeing. I'd never forgotten that conversation because it was the only time that my grandma told me a scary story. As soon as I got off the phone, I realized that my Mama, in that moment, was not talking to her first granddaughter, she was talking to the woman she helped shaped in me. She was talking to the soldier she trained to walk for others. The soldier, that, like her, would walk no matter the weather, no matter the day, no matter the sacrifice to help others.

My grandmother placed a burden on me, not to forget to look out for the younger siblings and cousins in my family. To continue to walk in truth and not in deception. To not pretend that all is well when things are toxic. Her observation during our last conversation did not go unnoticed. It did not escape me. Her words were not a mere comment in passing. Mama intentionally gave me permission to not pretend, to not ignore, to always walk in truth. She was the only one in the family who had no interest in pretending. For Mama, only truth, in its most real and vulnerable expression, could bring us peace.

I did not bother to go to her funeral. I did not have the emotional strength to grieve amongst so much confusion and pretense. I understood her love and her request.

I think about that often – how I never got to hold her hand one more time. Never got to thank her properly for those walks, for those introductions, for fighting my maternal grandmother to claim me every time she could.

For walking five kilometers in the heat of day to pick me up when no one else would.

For seeing me when I desperately needed to be seen.

The day Mama died was the day I lost my connection to my paternal family. Without her steady presence, the complex dynamics that she'd held together began to fragment. The gatherings became less frequent. The phone calls stopped. The family that had enveloped me in that swirling vortex of love scattered into separate corners of the world, became strangers with the passage of time.

I understand now that she wasn't merely walking to pick me up, but she was walking to save me. She was showing me what love looked like in motion – literal, physical, exhausting motion.

She was teaching me that love walks.

Decades later, when I ran that first 5K in my wedding gown for Gladys Ricart, I thought about Mama. When I walked 1,300 miles from New Jersey to Florida, I thought about her every single day.

I thought about how she walked for me when I couldn't walk for myself.

How she moved her massive, ailing body across kilometers of Dominican roads simply because I needed her.

She taught me that sometimes the most radical act of love is just showing up. Putting one foot in front of the other. Refusing to let distance, illness, or family drama stop you from claiming the people you love.

Mama's walks taught me everything I needed to know about advocacy, about showing up, about fighting for those who need to be seen.

She taught me that love doesn't ask for permission.

Love doesn't wait for convenient transportation.

Love doesn't let obstacles – physical, familial, financial – become excuses.

Love simply walks.

The memory nudges at me: my grandmother sitting at the head of her dining room table, Bible open, coffee steaming beside it.

That memory leads me to my own kitchen and my cozy sofa now, where I use my *cafetera* to brew that same strong coffee and read the same Words she used to read.

The ritual matters – gathering the ingredients, turning on the stove, finding the brown sugar, pouring the coffee into one of my favorite mugs. Each movement brings me back to that dining room where I'd sit with her and share moments of laughter, sometimes pain, but always love.

Sometimes I find my young daughter Sophia watching my every move, the way I once watched Mama.

I can still hear her voice: "*Mija, bébase un chin de café.*" Daughter, drink a little coffee.

And I do.

I drink, and I remember.

I remember that before I learned to walk for others, someone walked for me.

Before I understood what it meant to fight for visibility, someone fought to make me visible.

Before I knew that love could be loud and defiant and relentless, Mama showed me exactly what that looked like.

She showed me by walking.

Over and over and over again.

Until the day she couldn't walk anymore.

FIVE
You Don't Have To Be Like Your Mother

The sandwich tasted like disappointment.

Two slices of Wonder Bread. Yellow Kraft American cheese – the kind that came individually wrapped in plastic. Mayo spread thin across the soft white bread that stuck to the roof of my mouth.

I was eleven years old, fresh off a plane from Santo Domingo, sitting in my mother's one-bedroom apartment in Miami while she watched me eat. Waiting for me to say it was good. Waiting for gratitude.

I chewed slowly. The bread was too sweet. The cheese tasted like plastic. Nothing tasted like the food Abuela made back home – her rich blend of sofrito with garlic and red onions, *Ay Dios mío*, so good!

"*¿Te gusta?*" Mom asked. Do you like it?

I nodded. She smiled.

The lie was easier than the truth: that I wanted to go home. That Miami in 1983 wasn't the America I'd imagined. That the ocean here was murky and gray instead of turquoise. That the apartment smelled like flowery carpet powder and something else – something I couldn't name yet but would learn to recognize as fear.

The brown carpet was truly depressing. The walls were thin. I'd noticed the dents and holes while Mom had made my sandwich. Evidence of fists. Of bodies thrown against plaster. Of violence I didn't yet understand but would come to know intimately.

The space grew darker each night with the setting sun, and the light bulbs seemed to have less energy than the ones back in the DR.

Music became my escape.

I'd put on headphones and disappear into the bass lines, the lyrics, anything that could drown out the sounds coming from the next room. The shouting. The crashes. Arguments erupting like wildfire. The sick thud of fist against flesh.

Lionel Richie's smooth voice, Anita Baker's soulful cries – they became my shields.

That was until the bedroom door swung open and the violence between my mother and her boyfriend spilled into the living room, where they had tucked my cot away in a corner. I wasn't told that I wouldn't have a bedroom, but that did not seem as important after watching him hurt my mother, almost daily.

I squeezed my eyes shut, but the image seared itself onto my eyelids: his hands gripping my mother's arms, lifting her off the ground as his fist connected with her face. The impact vibrated through the cheap pressed wood floor under the carpet, a tremor that ran up my legs.

I felt the shudder of the walls as he slammed her head against the drywall. Prince on the big screen, his flamboyant performance in Purple Rain, became a strange mirror.

My mother's boyfriend – the man who should have been safeguarding us – was my tormentor. The monster under my bed. Except he wasn't under the bed. He was at the dinner table. In the living room. Always there.

Years stretched into a repeating cycle: the blows, the humiliation, the suffocating oppression of her emotional silence. I sat in the front row of every confrontation, a captive audience to a horror show playing out night after night.

And every day, she wore makeup like armor, taking hours sometimes. Foundation thick enough to hide the bruises. Powder to set it in place. Concealer under her eyes where the fingerprints showed. I watched her transform herself every morning, this performance of normalcy that fooled no one.

I learned to do the same. Not to cover bruises, but to cover shame. Every morning, makeup becomes my armor against the bad decisions I've made, the places I've been, the girl I was. Shame has been my biggest wound.

Sometimes we'd escape to her girlfriend's house to hide. A few days of peace. Then back to the apartment like nothing had happened. Like we hadn't just fled for our lives.

We always returned.

The Coral Gables police knew our address by heart. They'd show up, look bored, tell him to "take a walk." He'd leave in the small gray Chevy sedan she owned, whose back seat became my furnace – the only transportation she had to get to work. And the cycle would start again.

My stomach churned – a constant knot of confusion and fear. One minute I'd be wrestling with the conjugation of a new verb; the next, tears would stream down my face – a scream against the onslaught of puberty's hormonal tidal wave.

I was constantly watching my mother sink under the weight of repeated job losses, the financial stress creating a constant sense of despair, and ultimately, succumbing to a few grams of cocaine. Lost in her room for days, wearing shame instead of makeup, unable to make eye contact, trying to look sober and composed as she prepared herself a snack after days of not eating.

But she would always take him back.

The reconciliations were worse than the fights. The forced apologies. The Gladiolus. The pretending. I became indifferent, sarcastic, despondent. A teenager drowning in trauma I had no language to name. And there was more to come.

I was thirteen when the sitcom laugh track became background noise to something else entirely.

Summer was ending. The school bell would ring again soon. Bedtime was near, but I was watching TV, the flickering blue light painting stripes across my face.

He was on the other end of the sofa. Unusual. He usually watched his loud TV in his room. My skin prickled with a feeling I couldn't name as his bare feet, surprisingly cold, inched closer against my bare legs. A slow, deliberate creep.

I was too scared to look at him. Instead, I nervously adjusted my position on the sofa and turned my eyes to see what he was doing. My heartbeat doubled its pace, but my lungs fell behind as if it forgot to breathe.

The movement was jerky and frantic. I recognized it – a warped reflection of things I'd witnessed in the adult films he'd taken us to see. The familiar yet utterly alien movements mirrored scenes played out on screen so many times before.

The silence stretched. I froze, too scared to move.

When he finally stopped, the abrupt end felt as shocking as the event itself. I clicked the remote. The sudden darkness was a flimsy shield against the rising tide of something terrible.

My body reacted – a familiar physical response yet utterly divorced from any feeling of pleasure. The overwhelming shame took my breath away.

Years later, working with victims of sexual violence, I would learn what I couldn't name at thirteen: a child's body responds to stimuli regardless of consent. Pleasure and disgust can coexist, leaving a confusion that festers for decades. Your body remembers every touch, every fingerprint. The shame doesn't end with childhood – it follows you into consensual adult relationships, making you feel filthy, driving you toward riskier behaviors in a desperate attempt to feel something different, to reclaim some false sense of control. The cruel irony: those behaviors often aren't your real desires at all, just another layer of trauma. More shame. More condemnation. More pain.

A wave of self-loathing crashed over me in my room, the locked door a soft barrier against a world that felt suddenly, horribly wrong.

The panic attacks returned. Relentless. A deep, abiding sense of worthlessness. My body became a constant source of shame. Intimacy became synonymous with disgust, forever stained by the blue light of the television – a permanent scar in my memory.

To this day, I cannot sleep in a room with the TV on. I've gotten my own hotel room rather than share space with a lover, a friend, a family member who needs that blue flickering light. Some triggers never fade. I have been able to process and unpack most of my childhood traumas; and I am careful not to surround myself with its energy by unnecessarily entertaining known triggers.

Upgrade to the Fontainebleau apartment, though more spacious, offered a different kind of confinement. To afford the higher rent, I watched Mom disappear into the iconic Rusty Pelican restaurant, where she worked as a server. She seemed so happy each night as she counted out fat wads of cash – tips she spoke of with a bright, almost manic gleam in her eyes.

Those moments – watching her face light up as she fanned out twenty-dollar bills on the kitchen counter – I'd see glimpses of who she could be. A woman who worked hard. Who provided. Who smiled.

Then her boyfriend would appear, and the money would disappear into his pockets. Her smile would fade. The cycle would begin again.

I wanted to hate her. Some days I did. But mostly I just watched, trying to understand how someone could work so hard and give it all away. Trying to understand how love could look like this.

I didn't know I was learning a pattern I'd repeat. Didn't know I was memorizing the steps to a dance I'd perform with my own partner years later.

After his abuse, he would then offer an outing to the movies. The famous Miracle Mile theater loomed – an imposing structure that held the promise of escape but delivered only a deeper sense of dread. The old seats felt sticky with unspoken horrors. Forced into the lewd and dark space, I could feel his proximity as a physical assault. The aroma of popcorn couldn't mask the stench of shame.

The double feature – always that insidious pairing, the second film a grainy, grotesque perversion of sexual intimacy – played out on the screen while my body reacted, betraying its own horrors. A shudder, a flush, a wave of nausea... it was a language I didn't understand, a coded message from a past I didn't want to recall. Flashes of my previous sexual assaults at age 8 and 9.

The shame coiled around me. Mama's lessons on sin and spirituality haunted me – condemning me, my body, and my mind. But my fear of more violence against my mother forced me to remain still, stoic, and silent.

I was fifteen when I finally fought back.

Each step home from the bus stop felt like dragging myself through molasses. My stomach growled with hunger and my mouth dried with thirst. Carmen and Amaru – my only friends in eighth grade – were waiting for me. Our after-school ritual: riding bikes through the golf course, letting the sprinklers soak us at sunset.

I walked to Mom's apartment to pick up my bike and grab something to eat. My backpack thudded onto the worn carpet. I sat heavily on the old sofa and reached for the phone – that weighty beast of Bakelite – to confirm our plans.

Then I saw it.

His bedroom door – ajar. A sliver of pale skin. Then more.

He stood there, framed in the doorway. Naked. Glistening wet. Water dripped from his skin.

Rage slammed into me like a physical blow. Disgust, bitter in my mouth. Do not freeze. Do not freeze. I kept telling myself.

With strength I didn't know I possessed, I ripped the phone cord from the wall – the plastic snapping with a satisfying crack. The phone, still clutched in my hand, became a weapon. I swung it in a wild, desperate arc, aiming for him.

Did it hit him? I don't know.

All I knew was the need to run.

The Sweetwater Police Department sat directly across the street – its imposing presence mocking me with sterile calm. I burst through the doors, gasping for breath, my heart a frantic drum against my ribs.

A uniformed officer sat at the desk, his gaze fixed on something beyond me. His obliviousness was as familiar as my mother's. Without a word, I fled, once again feeling rejected. Unseen.

My legs carried me blindly toward the main road. I came upon Elio's Locksmith – its familiar sign a welcome sight in the overwhelming heat. The walk – a single block – felt like a lifetime.

A gentle smile greeted me. The young man behind the counter noticed the desperation on my face before gently allowing me to use the phone. My fingers fumbled with the plastic, cold against my clammy skin. Dialing Tía Doris's number, I held my breath.

She didn't answer.

A hand – large and calloused – rested on my shoulder. I flinched, then looked up into the worried face of the clerk.

"What's wrong?" he asked, his voice gentle.

My words tumbled out – a broken torrent of tears and a choked request: "Please... please, can you give me a ride to my friend's house?"

It was a quick ride. My body was so depleted and dehydrated I couldn't have walked another mile. Carmen and Amaru welcomed me with open arms, though their concern was obvious. Their older sister asked if I was okay. That's when I started sobbing.

As I told them what had just happened, they encouraged me to call my aunt again. They tried to distract and comfort me as I waited. We ordered pizza and talked about school, boys, our bike rides through the golf course at sunset.

Carmen's presence was soothing. Amaru's laughter and sarcastic way of finding humor in everything gave me hope.

Finally, Tía Doris picked me up.

Her voice, warm and gentle, reassured me: "You are safe with me." Tía Doris's embrace carried the scent of Oscar de la Renta, her favorite fragrance. I told her what had happened. She responded with a rapid-fire cascade of Spanish I could barely understand – but I knew she was cursing his name.

Tía contacted my mother, who was still living with him, and who then purchased a one-way ticket for me to return to the Dominican Republic. I was 15 years old, and I did not see mom or speak to her after the incident.

The airline logo seemed unfriendly before my eyes, blurring with the sudden, icy sting of tears. Rejection was no longer just a word. Rejection became the norm. My mother rejected me, focusing on her lover. My grandmother rejected me, focusing on her anger towards grandpa, who focused more on his alcohol and extra marital affairs than anything else. My Dad was busy with his own lover, having children, and not checking on my wellbeing. I felt rejected by those who were closest to me…I just felt rejected.

It was the coldness of that ticket, heavy in my hand – a physical manifestation of my mother's disbelief. Her abandonment.

The years leading up to that moment unraveled in my mind like a reel of fractured images: My grandmother's voice – *"No eres suficiente."* Not enough. The filthy and inappropriate touch of my relatives. The neighbor's violation at age nine. The stunned silence at dinner tables. The brutal psychological and physical abuse of my mother's boyfriend, his shadow looming, grooming, hoping that I would join him recreating some of the sexual scenes he exposed me to, his abuse a festering wound. My mother's own neglect – a constant, gnawing emptiness.

SIX
The First Escape

At seventeen, I couldn't recognize my own reflection.

The girl in the mirror was a stranger. No sense of self. No sense of belonging. Just the awkward heaviness of adolescence mixed with trauma I still couldn't name.

While living with Tia Doris, I started working as a Housekeeper at a local golf resort that hosted one of the most prestigious golf tournaments in Miami. I was proud to have this job. The ability to receive a paycheck that could help pay for my graduation expenses was humbling. Add to that the exposure to the elite.

The older women, mostly Hispanic and very kind, tried to warn me about Mike – the hardworking tech guy with expensive cologne and fancy jewelry. He was very attractive and always found me in the cafeteria. "He's known to prey on young staff," the ladies told me. I could sense the worry in their glances.

But I was seventeen, reckless, and desperate to feel something other than filthy. There was nothing threatening in his brown, sad eyes.

He asked me out. I said yes without thinking.

"Where do you want to go?" I asked.

"It's a surprise."

That slow smile. Eyes that never quite met mine. I thought it was shyness.

I was wrong.

❦

The Camaro was brand new. Red, gleaming under the streetlights. I'd never been in a car that nice. Never been to a restaurant where the waiter pulled out my chair.

We parked by the airport afterward to watch planes land. He had questions. I had too many answers.

I told him everything about my mother. No filters. The arrests. The drugs. The violence. Like I was talking to a girlfriend I didn't have. Like confessing would create intimacy instead of giving him a blueprint for how to break me.

"What's your favorite drink?"

"Amaretto." The word dissolved in my mouth. I'd tasted it once from Tía Doris's tiny bottle. Had no idea what I was saying yes to.

"Ever tried cocaine?"

The question hung between us. Casual. Like he was asking about the weather.

"No," I said. Then added: "One day I will get fucked up, so she sees what she does to me when she gets high."

The words of a wounded teen trying to sound brave. Trying to sound vindictive. Not realizing I was sitting across from a drug dealer who'd just been handed an instruction manual.

That same night, he dropped me at a fast-food restaurant. "Wait here," he said. "I'm picking something up."

He came back with a small bag of white powder.

I knew what it was the moment he handed it to me. I wasn't a stranger to cocaine. I'd watched my mother chase that high my entire childhood.

The first time I snorted it, I felt nothing. We were in his car. He told me what to do, rolled a dollar bill and showed me how to do it. Told me to take it slow.

But I was angry. Wanted to feel something immediately. Wanted to understand what had taken my mother from me. What was so amazing about drugs that a woman would choose them over her own child?

Seventeen wasn't a long life. But I'd already lived enough to know: I was looking for answers in all the wrong places.

What started as dates became something else.

Fancy shows at the Fontainebleau Hilton. Miami was still enjoying the reputation of magnates – drug dealers with pretty girls on their arms, fancy cars, lots of jewelry. Watching shows while showing her off like another accessory.

He bought me clothes for the shows – outfits that were revealing and appropriate for nightlife but inappropriate for a seventeen-year-old. Low-cut tops. Short skirts. I felt sophisticated. Didn't realize I was being packaged.

After the shows, we'd check into a motel where I'd stay for days with drugs, missing school, not telling Tía Doris where I was. He'd carry on with his life. His job. His family.

Yes, his family. Wife. Two sons. Something I found out months later from one of the housekeepers who finally worked up the courage to tell me.

The revelation should have been my wake-up call. Instead, I felt nothing. I was indifferent. I cared little about anything or anyone, including me.

During this time in my life, I was completely disassociated from reality. This was the only way for me to cope with everything I was experiencing. The less I felt the less I cared. No feeling no pain, no pain no shame. It is easier to do what is wrong when you don't have the ability to feel remorse. I hid behind my trauma to become indifferent and succumb to drugs. I never saw a way out. I did not think at 17 years old that I had a way out.

When he wasn't with me, I'd think about my mother. About the mirror I was becoming. The same shame. The same cycle. Different man, same trap. The haze of marijuana smoke blurred the line between right and wrong, between my will and his.

He was my dealer. My lover. My abuser.

Sometimes gentle. Sometimes… not.

Tía Doris gave me an ultimatum: stop seeing Mike or move out.

He rented me an efficiency within days. At the time, I thought he was being generous. Didn't understand that isolation is a weapon. That removing me from family oversight put me exactly where he wanted me.

Seventeen years old. Not yet graduated. Alone.

I missed school regularly. Was never sober enough to work. Lost weight. Sometimes didn't have much to eat unless I called him. The efficiency became a prison with pretty curtains.

Some days I'd stand in front of the mirror and not recognize myself. Hollow cheeks. Dark circles under my eyes. Bruises in various stages of healing – purple fading to green fading to yellow.

I looked like the women who'd shuffled through my mother's life at all hours. Desperate. Defeated. Eyes that had learned not to see.

I was becoming her.

The worst part wasn't the drugs or the violence. It was the slow death of hope. Each day that passed made it harder to remember I'd once dreamed of something different. The girl who'd arrived from Santo Domingo with stars in her eyes felt like someone else's story.

Paola picked me up one Saturday night. My childhood friend who understood. She had a rough childhood too. Was living on her own, trying to find a better life.

We partied until 6:00 AM. Danced until our feet hurt. Laughed until we forgot why we were sad.

I came home to find Mike had changed the locks.

Furious and hungover, we drove to the airport. He was boarding a plane to visit relatives overseas. The terminal was crowded with early morning travelers. I saw him in line to check in, that triumphant smile already on his face.

"Give me the keys, Mike. Why did you change the lock?"

"Because I pay the rent." He responded with a dash of toxic masculinity.

The keys hung around his neck on a lanyard. He expected this confrontation. Set the trap. Waited for me to walk into it.

I reached for the keys. He shoved me so hard I went down. The floor was cold against my back. People staring. An out-of-body moment – watching myself sprawled on airport tile while strangers formed an unwilling audience.

He grabbed my arm with his carry-on in the other hand, hauled me up, pushed me away from the crowd. I tried to break free. He dropped his suitcase and used both hands to throw me down again. Started punching.

Paola tried to pull him off, but she wasn't able to stop him.

Only the airport police got him off me.

I couldn't get up right away. Laid there for a few minutes watching myself try to make sense of something senseless. Something so humiliating I felt disgusted by the girl on the floor. Ashamed of her. Repulsed by her.

The police picked up his luggage. Told him to go. Looked at me and asked me to leave too.

No questions. No investigation. It was 1989. Five years before the O.J. Simpson case would change how domestic violence was prosecuted in America.

I returned to the apartment and spoke to the landlord. She said she'd give me access but I had to move out within a week. She'd heard the arguments. The beatings. She counseled me, encouraged me to get away from him. She was kind, but she also wanted me out.

A black eye greeted me the following morning. I looked in the mirror and saw my mother staring back.

I was seventeen. Almost eighteen.

I was her.

Without Mike and drugs, I did the only other thing I knew to do, I went to school. A teacher noticed the bruise and took me to the school counselor. My walk to her office was evidence of a violent weekend.

I remember her office. The lights were dimmed, but the lady in the office stood up. She invited me in as if she had been waiting for me. She asked me to take a seat and didn't close the door, which gave me peace and made me feel able to get up and walk out if I needed to.

"What are your plans after graduation?"

There was no question about the black eye. Rather about plans. Future. Words that felt like they belonged to someone else.

"What are your dreams?"

Dreams were for other girls. Girls with stable homes and parents who came to teacher conferences. Girls who didn't have to choose between paying rent and eating. Girls who weren't addicted to cocaine at seventeen.

But something about her patient eyes made the words tumble out. My mother. The drugs. The arrests. The violence. The man in the efficiency who paid my rent and bruised my face. Years of pain distilled into a shaky, rambling confession.

She listened. Didn't interrupt. Didn't look shocked or disgusted. Then she said the nine words that changed everything:

"You do not have to be like your mother."

Simple, yet devastating. Permission to imagine something different. But if I am not going to be like my mother, who was I to be like?

I was behind on credits from all the missed classes. This woman, I never met before, she made phone calls. Arranged night classes. Gave me Mr. Lindsey's name and number – someone at Miami Dade College who could help me enroll. Made sure I had everything I needed to graduate on time.

She became my advocate in a system that had mostly ignored me. Fought for me when I couldn't fight for myself. She did her job and by doing so changed my life. I learned from her that by doing my job I too, could change people's lives. This has become a guiding principle deeply engrained within my work ethics.

I found another apartment. Smaller. Cheaper. Applied at Denny's on Bird Road and 87th.

Mr. David, the manager, barely glanced at the bruise under my eye.

"Can you start next week?"

His lack of judgment felt like grace. Like maybe I wasn't as broken as I thought.

At a Buy Here Pay Here car dealership I bought a small car. The interest rates were outrageous – probably illegal – but without credit, it was my only option. I needed transportation. Needed independence. Needed to believe I could build something different.

I felt like I was finally starting to find myself. Create my own space. Have true friends at school and work.

But Mike kept showing up. At school. At work. Relentless.

I ignored him. Tried to.

My mother had been arrested again a few weeks earlier. Mike had offered to lend me the $150 bond money for the Women's Detention Center on 14th Street. Now he wanted it back.

He followed me to my new apartment one night. I made the mistake of arguing with him instead of calling the police. Made the mistake of letting him inside.

He was disturbed by my ability to say no now. No to his drugs. No to his gifts. No to his invitations to fancy shows and restaurants.

I'd found excuses – the full-time job, the college plans, my determination to stay clean.

But he didn't care about my excuses. He wanted to re-enter my life with full authority and control, just like before.

The argument escalated. My "no" meant nothing. My boundaries meant nothing. I accused him of stalking me. He said he wanted his money, started saying derogatory things about me and my mother.

I tried to stay calm. Knew it was escalating. Knew it wouldn't end well.

I was in the cramped kitchen trying to do dishes when I felt his hands grab my hair. Shoved me toward the ground. I kept my balance but he locked my head with his left forearm. Started punching with his right fist.

I hit his back with my right arm. Trying to get him to stop. Trying to breathe. My left hand reached out to ground myself, landing on the kitchen counter.

Life handed me an invitation when my hand found the butcher knife handle.

Cool steel. My fingers wrapped around it comfortably, like it belonged there.

The choice crystallized with devastating clarity: I could end his life.

The rage was familiar. I remember feeling the same heat I'd felt one night in which I fought my own mother. That power. That righteous indignation that scared me more than his fists ever could.

Memories flickered through my oxygen-starved brain. News reports from my Miami childhood. Spanish-language broadcasts detailing stabbings. The precise placement of a blade for maximum damage. I'd absorbed more than I realized.

I knew how to do this.

The presence of it in my hand was oddly reassuring. One movement. That's all it would take.

Instead, I used every drop of strength and flung it as far away from me as I could.

He stopped, released his grip. For a moment, we were frozen, the only sound my ragged breathing. I could feel his eyes on me as my body and face were still facing the floor, slowly collapsing towards the ground.

Without getting up or laying eyes on him, I managed to say, "Get the fuck out of my house because next time, if there is a next time, I will kill you."

As I heard the door slam shut, my body began to shake uncontrollably. I stayed on that cold floor for hours, weeping for my dignity, grieving my self-respect, and wondering if this was the mud, again.

For months, his stalking became relentless. My coworkers saw the bruises and injuries which I had learned to hide with makeup. Still my mother.

12 hours at work, I was a nervous wreck: entering the wrong order, screaming at the cook, constantly agitated at every beep of my pager.

My coworkers walked me to my car only to find four flat tires. Mike. I had enough tips to fix. But the next day, after another 12-hour shift, the car wouldn't start. He had put something in the gas tank that completely ruined the engine.

I went back in the restaurant, sat in Mr. David's office. In tears I told him, "I quit, I can't work here anymore." He gave me a ride home and told me to rest. I slept for a long time. After a day off, I asked Mr. David if I could return to work. He said yes.

The next morning was one of the most beautiful displays of love I ever experienced from coworkers. We did not talk about my car. All we did was crack jokes, ate pancakes, and drank coffee. The entire overnight crew, including Mr. David.

Later, Jennifer pulled me aside, her face etched with concern. "You're staying with me," she said, her voice low and firm.

Her one-bedroom apartment in Coconut Grove became my sanctuary. I shared space with her six-year-old son, grateful for the safety of their small home.

Only years later did I learn the truth: Mr. David had slipped money into Jennifer's hand to cover her rent for the month. The same man who'd hired me despite the black eye had quietly made my rescue possible.

My coworkers circled me like protective birds. They saw the exhaustion mixed with terror in my eyes. They acted.

Each day in Jennifer's apartment, the fear receded a little. The fragile cocoon held.

He continued to stalk me, but I was emotionally stronger now and would just ignore him.

I saw him twice as an adult. He didn't recognize me.

The first time was at a supermarket around 2002. He walked right next to me. Nothing. I was invisible to him.

The second time, maybe 2004, I was meeting a female judge at the Capital Grille on Brickell Avenue. I saw him setting up audio visual equipment in a private dining area. I had to pass him to reach the main dining room.

I was no longer the innocent seventeen-year-old he tried to destroy and almost succeeded. I was a woman in a tailored business suit, college degree, high heels, long wavy hair, radiating confidence.

But here's the thing: Mike had many Josies. I only had one Mike.

I never forgot his height, his hairy arms, how he walked and smiled. I could sense his aura in a room even if I didn't see him. He either didn't see me or pretended not to.

I never saw him again after that.

He continued to stalk me, but I was emotionally stronger now and would just ignore him.

I graduated high school in 1990. Eighteen years old. Carrying more raw knowledge and substance than any diploma could measure.

I'd survived childhood sexual abuse. Immigration. My mother's boyfriend's violence and assault. My mother's addiction and arrests. Teen dating violence. Cocaine. Isolation.

The survival skills I'd developed – the hypervigilance, the ability to read danger in someone's posture or tone, the determination to keep moving forward no matter what – would become both my greatest strengths and my deepest wounds.

That fall, thanks to my school guidance counselor, I started college at Miami Dade. Worked full-time at Denny's. Lived in my tiny efficiency. Drove my second overpriced car with its predatory interest rate.

Eighteen. Alone. Determined.

The counselor's words became my mantra: You do not have to be like your mother.

I wanted to walk toward something else. Something better.

And so, my first escape wasn't just from Mike.

It was from a cycle I'd been born into. A pattern that stretched back through generations of women in my family who'd learned to survive but not to live. From the belief that violence and chaos were all I deserved. From the girl who looked at herself and saw only her mother's reflection.

From every message that told me I was disposable. Controllable. Unworthy of safety or peace. That my body existed for other people's pleasure or violence. That saying no was dangerous. That love looked like control.

I was learning, slowly and painfully, that I could be someone else. Someone new.

The cost would be high. Years of therapy I couldn't yet afford. Relationships I'd sabotage before they could hurt me. A body that carried the memory of every blow, every violation, every moment I'd been made to feel small.

But at eighteen, with my high school diploma and my Denny's uniform and my Buy Here Pay Here car, I was beginning to understand something crucial:

Escape was possible.

Not easy. Not clean. Not complete. Not immediate.

But possible.

And when you're drowning, possible is enough to keep swimming.

Years later, I would walk 1,300 miles in my wedding dress for Gladys Ricart. For every woman who tried to leave and was struck down for it.

But that walk started here.

In that Miami kitchen with a knife in my hand and a choice to make.

In that school counselor's office where someone finally saw me and gave me permission to imagine a different future.

In the Denny's break room where my coworkers circled me like protective birds.

In the constant presence of my aunt Doris and my cousin Leo's calls.

In every step I took away from that efficiency apartment toward something I couldn't yet name but desperately needed to find.

My first escape was choosing to fling instead of stab.

Choosing to walk away instead of becoming him.

Choosing to believe the counselor's words even when I couldn't yet see the path forward.

Choosing to let my coworkers help me when independence had always meant isolation.

That was my first walk toward healing.

There would be many more to come.

SEVEN
Knock & Talk

But I'm getting ahead of myself. Before Mike. Before the knife in my hand. Before I learned to scream instead of stab.

There was my mother's final betrayal.

The arrival of the one-way ticket from my mother felt like rejection, but it was also a lifeline.

I didn't need to be around drugs, my mother, or her boyfriend. I lived in the Dominican Republic for about a year with my grandparents again.

Abuela's tiny kitchen was her haven of quiet chaos. I would watch her hands, dried and worn from years of hard labor, moving with relentless energy as she prepared food for others, always putting their needs before her own. Her sad smile, a barely-there curve of her lips, spoke volumes more than words ever could. I watched her selflessness, and it felt really moved by it.

It was different this time. I met a gentler abuela – or maybe I just saw her differently.

Within a year, my mom asked me to return to the States.

I was overwhelmed with joy. I felt redeemed, loved, wanted. She misses me. She's choosing me instead of him.

But upon arrival, I learned the truth.

The slam of the front door. The familiar scent of stale cigarette smoke and something else – something acrid and sharp. Crack cocaine had entered my mother's home.

Mom's face was pale, her eyes glazed over. There was a constant stream of strangers through the house: doctors, wealthy moms, lawyers, even a few from the Indian reservation who were regular clients.

Now my mom was both dealer and user.

One afternoon, after walking home from school, I entered an unusually clean and tidy apartment.

The scent of lemon polish, carpet powder, and stewed chicken completely confused my senses. Everything was too neat – the sofa cushions plumped to impossible perfection, the dishes stacked precisely.

My mom's meticulous cleaning felt like a premonition I didn't understand until the sharp rap-rap-rap of knuckles on the door.

BAM.

The sound echoed in my chest, the door shuddering under the force. "Police!" The voice was flat, authoritative, cutting through the unnatural quiet.

My mother's hand, quick and frantic, fumbled at the doorknob. But the officer, a wall of muscle in a plain t-shirt, shoved past her with the casual brutality of a bulldozer clearing a path.

I felt resentment growing in my throat as my untouched dinner sat cooling on the coffee table. Sixteen, and I still looked twelve. No makeup, no heels, just jeans and a band t-shirt – the uniform of adolescence, not a hardened criminal.

Their "knock and talk" was their excuse.

My mom's voice, usually a warm alto, became a frantic shriek. Her hands, usually gentle, lashed out. The click of metal handcuffs was brutally sudden, sharp against the silence.

The sight of her wrists encircled in metal, the fear in her eyes – the taste of my dinner soured in my mouth, my appetite draining away.

The officer, his face impassive, gestured for me to stay put. "Just a couple of hours," he mumbled, the words as hollow as the promise they contained.

Years later, the police report detailed it all: the glimpse of a small scale on the dining room table, a detail lost in that day's chaos. Enough, apparently, for a warrant.

Six hours stretched into an eternity of my mother's desperate curses, fervent prayers, and heart-wrenching sobs.

The narcotics unit's arrival was a spectacle of controlled chaos. Flashlights sliced through the gloom, their movements precise and unsettling. Then came the discoveries: the drugs, bagged and tagged; the gun, cold and metallic; and finally, the dildo, displayed in all its shocking, humiliating detail.

I watched as officers laid out their evidence – a cruel and grotesque exhibit for me to witness. They must have thought I was used to it, but I wasn't.

At that point in my life, I had never held drugs. My mother never shared drugs with me or allowed me to see her using. I saw her high many times, but never using in front of me, never.

The final act that evening: the arrival of HRS, now known as the Department of Children and Families. They asked about relatives, and I could only mention my aunt, Tía Doris – she was my only relative in Florida. They contacted her to pick me up because my mother was being taken to jail.

I heard my mom trying to talk to the detective.

The handcuffs clicked cold against her wrists, I could see how tight it was against her wrist. She had convinced the cops to let her shoulders rest by handcuffing her hands in the front instead of the back. Her eyes, usually bright and teasing, were dull with fear.

"Please," she mumbled to the officers, her voice barely a whisper thick with exhaustion, "just let me get something for my daughter from the kitchen."

A stiff-lipped officer nodded, and I watched, numb, as she handed me a small, soft toy in the form of a cat. Its fur was matted, one button eye dangling precariously. It felt strangely heavy in my hands, but I took it trying not to show how awkward I felt.

I was never into stuffed animals. Mom knew that. I didn't understand why she would give me a stuffed cat.

With tears streaming down her face, mom apologized. Not just a simple apology, but a gut-wrenching, heartbroken confession spoken directly to me, a 16-year-old child who should have been shielded from all the ugliness of her behaviors, choices, and actions.

The officer's gaze was cold, and my mom's trembling voice was swallowed by my sudden, crushing fear. "Take care of yourself, *mija*," she said, her voice thick with unshed tears. "We'll be together soon."

Tía Doris's apartment became my sanctuary once again. I crawled into the familiar bed, the sheets stiff and scratchy against my skin, and slept the sleep of exhaustion, not peace.

The next few days blurred into a frantic rush of phone calls. I watched Tía Doris, her face etched with worry lines I hadn't noticed before, pacing the tiny apartment, her phone pressed to her ear, her voice tight with strained patience as she pleaded with someone on the other end.

I saw the desperation in her eyes as she searched through drawers, counting crumpled bills, responsibility crushing her shoulders. The burden of my mother's actions pressed down on us. The familiar shame burned in my throat. Anxiety and cold sweats began taking over my body.

My aunt's shoulders slumped under the burden of our family's lack of resources. We had nothing. No safety net.

News reports from the Dominican Republic flashed through my mind – images of overcrowded cells, squalid conditions, desperate faces – a terrifying vision of where my mother might end up.

Each passing day stretched into eternity, seconds ticking by like lead weights. Finally, after what felt like forever, the bondsman arrived, a hulking figure who seemed to materialize from thin air, and the agonizing wait in the cold, sterile waiting room began as we waited for mom's release.

Hours bled into one another, each minute a reminder of the vulnerability that had opened between us.

The relief when the heavy steel door finally swung open to release my mother was bittersweet. The whirlwind of recent days – the bail hearing, the hushed whispers, the frantic phone calls – left me dizzy and disoriented.

Seeing mom walk through those imposing jail doors should have brought relief, a wave of pure joy. Instead, I felt annoyed and ready to go home and sleep. I was relieved, but I was also allowing myself to be angry.

We went to Tía's apartment instead of taking mom directly home. I had made it clear that I would not return to living with my mother under any circumstances, with or without her boyfriend.

Mom didn't seem bothered – her bright and teasing look had returned, and she was more arrogant than ever before.

The aroma of simmering chicken and rice couldn't mask the underlying tension. I craved sleep, a deep, restorative slumber to wash away the exhaustion, but my hope flickered and died with Mom's first words.

"Someone set me up," she announced, her voice low and dangerous, a glint in her eye. "And now I know how to play the game."

Those words hit my subconscious like an axe thrown in my direction. What game? What setup? My mind raced like a frantic hamster on a wheel.

Before I could unravel the mystery, Mom's voice cut through my thoughts. "My stuffed cat," she said, her intense gaze fixed on me with strange urgency. "The one I gave you."

"The tattered, floppy-eared thing I clutched and took to school while you were locked up? That cat?"

This cat represented a vulnerable moment we shared, a tangible link to her, something I'd kept safe, believing it held some precious, unspoken message.

I went to the room, my heartbeat irregular. Retrieving it from my school backpack, I returned and offered it to her silently.

The plush fabric felt strangely cold and filthy in my hands as I passed it over.

Then, with a swift, practiced movement, Mom sliced open the seam.

A small package wrapped in plastic tumbled onto the coffee table. Several off-white rock pieces, varying in size and shape, fell from the package; a few smaller bags with white powder scattered among the stuffing.

Tía Doris gasped. My jaw dropped.

Mom laughed – a harsh, brittle sound that shattered the fragile calm.

"Mom," I choked out, the words raw with pain and betrayal. "You used me? After everything...you used me?"

The dam broke.

Everything – the fear, the confusion, the crushing weight of betrayal – exploded. I don't remember how it started, only the furious energy coursing through me, the searing heat of anger.

Fists flew, feet connected, my hands pulled at her hair. It wasn't just punches and kicks; it was the raw, untamed fury of a betrayed child unleashed.

Tía Doris's hands were everywhere, pulling me away, her strength surprising. But my rage was a monster, wild and uncontainable.

Then came the icy shock of the shower.

Cold water hammered against my skin, sobs wracking my body. Tía held me tight, we were both fully dressed, her arms like a vise around me as icy water washed over us both. We clung together, two drenched, heartbroken figures, the cold water mirroring the chill that had settled deep within my soul.

Only when the storm inside me finally subsided, leaving a hollow ache in its wake, did Tía Doris gently lead me to bed.

They left me alone then, taking my mother to her apartment, leaving me with the lingering chill of the cold shower and the devastation of what had happened.

I couldn't sleep.

I started sobbing again – more like grieving. I just didn't know what I was grieving.

The kitchen was cold, linoleum tiles biting at my bare feet. My hand, trembling slightly, reached for the water pitcher. The glass filled slowly, halfway, then stopped.

The water, clear and innocent, seemed to mock me. Each drop felt heavy, like tiny lead weights dragging me further down.

A wave of exhaustion crashed over me – a bone-deep weariness that went beyond sleeplessness. It was a suffocating blanket of loneliness.

A bitter laugh caught in my throat – a cruel joke, this life, orchestrated by some unseen, malevolent force.

The thought, sharp and sudden, sliced through the fog: just end it.

I felt so tired, used, rejected, abandoned. Maybe abuela was right – I was useless, too emotional, too weak.

All I knew for certain was that I was 16: raped by a neighbor, molested by my mother's boyfriend, touched by family members, not acknowledged after Abuela took me to the hospital for injuries.

For a young girl already carrying too heavy a burden, the urge to simply cease existing was almost a provocative invitation.

Tía's promise echoed faintly, a fragile whisper against the deafening silence of my despair. The image of her car pulling away, my mother slumped in the back seat, played on repeat in my mind.

Used. The word burned like acid. Used by my mother, a burden to Tía Doris. The frantic efforts to free Mom from jail, the hope, the exhaustion – it all felt pointless. Foolish.

Like a macabre inheritance, the vision of following in her footsteps, my alcoholic grandfather footsteps, a life consumed by the same demons, rose sickeningly in my stomach.

God? The word was absent, a vacant space where faith should have been. Only a gaping void of betrayal remained.

My thoughts, sluggish and leaden, moved so slowly. My hand stopped trembling. I stood steady and, with chilling resolve, reached for the Clorox under the kitchen sink.

I watched, fascinated and detached, as the thick, yellowish liquid poured into the glass, swirling and mixing with the water – a clear, deceptively innocent mixture.

Did I want to die? Not exactly. But I didn't know how to live like this anymore. I did not know how else to stop the pain. I needed the pain to stop, immediately, I needed it to end.

Hopelessness pressed down like an anvil. The endless cycle of my mother's addiction, the neglect, the gut-wrenching betrayal of being used as a drug mule – it was all too much. This final indignity, the ultimate violation, was too much to bear.

I couldn't bear the hurt anymore.

That was the only thought that remained as I lifted the glass and drank.

I woke up at Jackson Memorial Hospital.

Mom was standing next to me.

A thick plastic tube snaked from my mouth – making it impossible to scream or beg her to leave.

Days blurred into a hazy, sterile landscape. The crisis unit. Walls closing in, each breath a reminder of the failure, the shame, the bullshit I had to endure daily.

I often wondered if I was the only real person. Was I in a sitcom? Was everyone else real, or was I the only one? The ability to dissociate and pretend that this was an out-of-body experience was easier to digest that living in the filthy reality I found myself in.

The silence between my mother and me was thick. No discussion about why I was in the hospital. No questions about my feelings, my healing plan, no let's-start-over conversation. No shared tears, no whispered apologies – I guess those were reserved for when she wore handcuffs.

Later, snippets of cruel laughter drifted to me from my cousin and some of his friends.

I had become the joke.

I saw their faces, twisted in mockery of pity or maybe just plain amusement. Color drained from my cheeks – not anger, but deep, bone-chilling shame.

A cold wave washed over me, leaving me numb, heavy, sunk beneath the gravity of their words, their knowing glances.

They didn't bother asking what was hurting me, so I didn't bother explaining.

We were teens – the only thing that mattered, or at least began to matter to most of us was: are we playing pool tonight, and who's getting the alcohol?

This was the girl who would meet Mike a year later.

Already used. Already betrayed. Already convinced she was worthless.

Already groomed for exploitation.

My mother had shown me exactly what I was worth: a container for her drugs. A shield for her consequences. A body to be used when convenient and discarded when not.

When Mike appeared with his red Camaro and his questions and his cocaine, I was already prepared to give myself away. My mother had taught me how.

The pattern was set. The lessons learned.

This is what daughters inherit when mothers choose drugs over everything else. Not just addiction. Not just trauma.

The belief that your body exists for other people's purposes. That your pain doesn't matter. That love looks like use.

Sixteen years old, fresh from a suicide attempt, mocked by family and friends, abandoned by my mother, and ignored by my father.

Already walking toward the next man who would hurt me.

Because I didn't know yet that I could walk away instead.

EIGHT
Trauma On Legs

I would often use my attitude, high heels, manicured nails, delicate makeup, and a friendly voice to convince myself and everyone else how great I was doing in most areas of my life.

At least once per week, my hair would be wavy and silky with a blowout that would make my curls bounce with every step I took.

Sooo trauma, what trauma?

I met Nico while working with the Florida Department of Juvenile Justice.

I pulled up to his home driveway on a Sunday morning to meet him for the first time, then we drove from South Florida to Tallahassee for Monday morning training. Six hours in a compact car the State of Florida was generous enough to let us rent – an insane way to meet a coworker for the first time.

We were both less than okay with the arrangement. We decided to endure the trip with the intention of hitchhiking or getting our own personal rental if things didn't work out. At least that was my plan – I never asked him if he had one.

Our work trip, which we both expected to be weird and uncomfortable, turned out to be the beginning of a great friendship.

Nico's parents are both from Greece, and he was born in Brooklyn, New York. His Mediterranean appearance always made him stand out. He was and continues to be married to his beautiful wife, with whom he shares three beautiful children. He has the ability to transform himself into a twelve-year-old boy in zero seconds and say the goofiest things with the face of a child.

At six feet tall with an athletic build and the sense of humor of a New Yorker – sharp and fast – Nico turned out to be a kind man with a big heart and an overwhelming love for life, his family, and his coworkers.

As a former Juvenile Offender Probation Officer, Nico had the approach of "pull up your pants, shut up, and sit down."

In his new role as a Technical Assistance Specialist, I was to train him how to teach and train others – office staff, probation officers, agencies that received funding from us – to accept the juvenile offender with unconditional positive regard.

Meaning, we were to meet the client where they were: saggy pants, cursing, disrespectful, or angry. Our job was to welcome them into our workspace when they showed up, regardless of their attitudes. Our job was to show them respect and acceptance and model the behavior for them even if they didn't deserve it or hadn't received it.

As long as safety was under control, the client's attitude was irrelevant to how we would treat them – always a young person under eighteen.

I used to take an enormous amount of pleasure every time I reminded him of our mission and vision.

We were both hired to do the same job, but we had different backgrounds. I was always an advocate and used a person-centered approach. However, Nico was, you know, Greek, from New York – respect and honor kind of guy. He has a master's degree in business, and he made it his business to make those young people respect him.

My job? To reprogram him to think differently about honor and respect when working with young people who happened to commit crimes and get caught in the criminal justice system.

Training Nico to use and embrace the idea of using a more empathic approach to work with juvenile offenders took me a precious amount of time and energy.

However, Nico redeemed himself for life with what I received from him during our journey together.

As we continued working together, Nico learned about some of my childhood trauma and health issues.

Every once in a while, my anxiety would limit my ability to teach a class or session, and Nico always had my back.

While working at the agency, I encountered several health issues, including two severe pulmonary embolisms that almost killed me, as well as severe anxiety and increased panic attacks without any perceived triggers. My health started to decline rapidly in 2013, and Nico introduced me to research that could explain some of my illness.

After about a year of working together, he invited me to attend a Child Network Conference on the Treasure Coast, which was the area he was assigned to.

The main workshop during the conference was research by the Centers for Disease Control and Kaiser Permanente: Adverse Childhood Experiences study. The Huffington Post article called it the "largest and most important public health study" – seventeen thousand people, fifteen years of their lives poured into charts and graphs, detailing health and trauma.

The workshop was detailed and very enlightening but also very triggering for me.

I managed to finish the session without leaving the room, but I can assure you that I did leave my body emotionally, which is a coping mechanism I used often.

Dissociation is one of the many coping skills that numerous trauma survivors use to endure moments in which our bodies become overly aroused with feelings and emotions.

For me, the emotion can be good or bad. Once I become overwhelmed, I panic, shut down, or become emotionally dysregulated.

I could be angry during an interaction where anger wasn't a reasonable response. For example, I was very angry and disappointed when I suffered my pulmonary embolism. Yes, I almost died, but I didn't die, and I had work to do and schoolwork.

If I didn't get the work done because I had to rest and recover, how could I then be worthy to live in society and community? I know this is an absurd example, but it's my real example, and most trauma reactions tend to be very absurd – one of the many reasons why many loved ones often fail to understand what a trauma survivor is trying to fight.

We are fighting to live and be seen, accepted, redeemed, loved without boundaries but with tremendous care. We don't want to be exploited; we want to be protected.

We don't always think that we deserve it because as children the message was that we deserved nothing, so as adults we want to prove ourselves.

I needed to prove myself. I didn't have time to be sad, anxious, or sick and about to die. My thought was either kill me or let me go to work and school because I have no time. Very, very, very graceless.

I didn't have an ounce of grace to offer to my sick body because my mind and emotions were also very sick.

Three years after Nico introduced me to the Adverse Childhood Experiences (ACE) study, I found myself in the training room at the Broward County Children's Advocacy Center.

There, I was working as a Mental Health Therapist for children who had been sexually and physically abused.

The entire staff, including me, prepared to receive an up-to-date and very personal look at the ACE study and how to utilize its assessment in real time.

The Sanctuary Institute facilitated the training to ensure that our agency would operate as a trauma-informed organization. Trauma-informed means that we approach everyone in the agency – clients and staff – as if they have experienced trauma.

The goal of the training was very noble and trendy in an era where healing trauma had become the next exploited social theme. However, during that time, I and a few other coworkers would go out of our way to hide our trauma, especially at work.

During this specific training, a strange energy began to fill the room as the facilitator offered some trigger warnings, which were very triggering to me.

The Sanctuary Model. Trauma-Informed Care. Great concept – so idealistic and even compassionate – and yet, we were daily so indifferent to our own trauma wounds in our day-to-day operations.

I walked the halls victoriously with my master's degree, license to practice mental health, to help others with their traumas, to advocate for victims of violent crimes, offering no compassion, information, or even acknowledgment of my own trauma wounds.

But on this day, I was unable to escape seeing the damage firsthand, quantified and scored.

I tried so hard to feel safe and calm, but every slide, every video, every "trauma-informed remark" had a hint of something else – a deep, unsettling recognition of our own unacknowledged childhood chaos.

More than twenty pairs of eyes, with anxious and expectant breathing, trying to do our best to hold it together.

I was hoping that the speaker was incompetent, boring even. I didn't want her to be compassionate and efficient. Her delivery could expose me, my wounds. I didn't want to be emotionally naked, for my coworkers to see my ugly wounds.

But my wish didn't come true. Within five minutes, I realized how skilled she was, and I was done – well, more like undone.

Shame, disgust, resentment, anger, self-pity, impostor syndrome – I experienced a lot during that training.

As we moved through the information, concepts, statistics, victim video testimonies, I started tasting blood, uncovering boils on my soul.

I wanted to run out of the room, but I would have had to walk in front of all my coworkers, bathed in shame and completely, utterly emotionally naked.

I stayed in the room instead.

No, I wasn't leaning into discomfort or trying to do the hard thing – I was frozen with terror. The terror of being seen in all my filth.

If day one had me on the edge, day two kicked me off the cliff, and I fell hard.

The entire class was asked to take the ACE assessment using our own trauma history.

Each question felt like removing an article of clothing. The process was excruciatingly painful and particularly cruel.

The questionnaire was designed to measure the impact of childhood abuse and neglect on our physical health and emotional well-being. Ten questions, yes or no answers – the more questions answered with a yes, the more likely the individual would experience severe health issues as an adult.

Eight out of ten.

Wait, nine out of ten.

Nine out of ten?

Wait, wait, let me do the math again.

Mind racing, inability to breathe, sweaty palms, heart beating fast, shame showering me mixed with sweat.

Let me read the questions again – maybe I'm being too harsh. I did the math again and again. I've never been confident in math; maybe I didn't add correctly.

But I have a master's degree, I told myself in desperation. Internal arguments in the midst of a panic attack were a common trend in my life.

I should know how to add from one to ten.

Nine out of ten?

The number left me defeated.

I remained looking at the paper, scanning the questions, trying to find a mistake on my part, but I couldn't find any. The only thing I could find were the many diagnoses that only confirmed my ACE score.

I felt sick.

Decades of digging, dumping, covering the past, burying the memories, digging deeper to hide more, only to have a "trauma-informed expert" expose me at the height of my professional career?

The silence that followed felt heavy enough to keep me immobile for hours.

My ACE score hit me hard. The numbers quantifying my own trauma, using the ACE questionnaire, left me disoriented.

As I examined the data, I felt like I had a physical weight on my chest.

Each statistic whispered violently: "this is your number, this is your identity, here is your score."

Success – a corner office, a car that purrs, a bank account that finally breathes – felt like a gilded cage.

I had it all and nothing at the same time.

The ghost of my mother's rage still echoed sometimes, a phantom limb twitching beneath the surface of my composure. A colleague's casual touch sent a jolt of unexpected panic through me. The forced smile I plastered on for my church family felt like a mask, thin and cracking.

In 2023, the U.S. Department of Health and Human Services reported that more than half a million children were abused and/or neglected by family members. But those are only the cases that were reported, investigated, and confirmed by authorities.

That same year, Child Protective Services received more than four million referrals involving over seven million children. Again – referrals. Reported. Known. Documented.

For those of us who have studied and worked inside the criminal justice system, we understand something else: the dark figure of crime. The cases that never make it into a report. The children who never disclose. The ones who, like me, did not feel seen, protected, or heard by the very systems designed to protect them.

The National Crime Victimization Survey attempts to account for that hidden number – to estimate the children who experienced abuse but never reported it to law enforcement. The children who stayed silent. The children who survived quietly.

The Centers for Disease Control and Prevention has stated that at least one in seven children in the United States experienced abuse or neglect in the past year. If the population of children under eighteen was approximately 73.3 million in 2023, that would mean closer to ten million children experienced abuse that year – not half a million.

Ten million.

Ten million fragile and developing brains absorbing trauma while still under construction.

When trauma enters a child's life, it does not simply create a bad memory. It disrupts neural development. It alters stress response systems. It interferes with the healthy wiring of emotional regulation.

Trauma interrupts the architecture of the brain.

It floods the nervous system with stress hormones, teaching the body that the world is unsafe. It freezes parts of development in place. It can leave a child emotionally younger than their chronological age – struggling to self-regulate, struggling to trust, struggling to attach securely.

And later, we wonder why there is chaos.

We wonder why relationships fracture. Why impulsivity surfaces. Why aggression or withdrawal become coping mechanisms.

But if ten million children a year are navigating trauma while their brains are still forming, then what we are witnessing in adulthood is often not pathology – it is adaptation.

Adaptation to survive environments that should have been safe.

This is the part that is hardest to grasp: that so many innocent, developing minds can be reshaped – even malfunction – not because they were broken, but because they were forced to survive what they should never have had to endure.

What does trauma look like on legs? I am glad you asked!

It looks functional. Productive. Driven. It looks like a woman in a wedding gown walking 1,300 miles from New Jersey to Miami. It looks like activism. It looks like purpose.

It looked like me.

Trauma is not always a child rocking in a corner. Sometimes it is a child who learns to move fast. To perform. To survive. To read every room before she enters it.

When a child grows up in chaos, the nervous system does not rest. It does not get to power down. The stress response – that ancient alarm system designed to protect us – stays switched on. Stress hormones flood the body over and over again, signaling danger even when the room is quiet. The body inflames. The heart races. The mind scans.

I did not know that as a child my brain was wiring itself around survival.

I just knew I could never relax.

The fight-flight-freeze response became my personality. I fought when cornered. I fled when intimacy felt too close. And sometimes I froze – dissociating, leaving my body long before I knew that word. I became hyper-aware of tone shifts, footsteps, silence. My amygdala – that tiny alarm system in the brain – behaved as if everything was a threat. A new relationship. A new opportunity. Even love.

When I watched the news on September 26, 1999, and saw that a bride – Gladys Ricart – had been murdered on her wedding day, something inside me shattered. I did not know her. But my nervous system did. It recognized danger. It recognized betrayal. It recognized the illusion of safety.

That is what trauma does. It bypasses logic and goes straight to the body.

When the stress response is chronically activated in childhood, it shapes development. The prefrontal cortex – the part of the brain responsible for impulse control, reasoning, planning – becomes dysregulated. Decisions are made from fear, not wisdom. I did not understand why I kept running toward relationships that felt intense instead of safe. Why shame drove me into beds I was not emotionally prepared to be in. Why I could testify before Congress but could not sit still alone in my own apartment without feeling restless.

My hippocampus – the brain's memory processor – stored my early experiences not as neat narratives but as fragments. Sensations. Smells. Songs. A shift in someone's voice could transport me back to childhood without warning. Trauma memories are often sensory, not chronological. The body remembers what the mind tries to forget.

To the outside world, a traumatized child may look defiant. Oppositional. Dramatic. But often what you are witnessing is dysregulation. A nervous system that never learned safety.

In my life, it manifested as hyper-independence. As emotional volatility. As difficulty trusting. As attachment patterns that swung between clinging and distancing. The very people I loved the most sometimes received the brunt of my dysregulated nervous system – including my daughters. That is one of the hardest truths to write.

When a child's primary source of safety is also the source of fear, attachment becomes disorganized. Love and danger intertwine. The nervous system never fully settles. As adults, this can surface as intimate partner violence, impulsivity, emotional reactivity, or criminal behavior rooted not in evil, but in unhealed survival wiring.

For years, my activism masked my dysregulation. Walking those miles in a wedding gown felt noble. It was noble. But it was also flight. I was running – not just toward justice – but away from myself.

Chronic childhood trauma does not only affect relationships. It imprints the body. Research, including the landmark Adverse Childhood Experiences Study, has shown strong links between early adversity and later depression, anxiety, substance abuse, heart disease, autoimmune disorders, obesity, and suicidality. The body keeps the score long after the mind minimizes the story.

This is difficult to conceive.

That the decisions of parents – their violence, their addictions, their neglect, their emotional absence – can transform an innocent brain still under construction. That a developing nervous system can be wired around fear instead of safety. That a child adapts so brilliantly to survive that those adaptations later become her greatest obstacles.

Trauma on legs looks like competence wrapped around chaos. It looks like shame disguised as ambition. It looks like a woman who changes laws but cannot yet soothe her own nervous system.

It looks like me – before I learned that survival is not the same as healing.

And healing required something far more difficult than walking 1,300 miles.

It required staying.

Forty-five years old, and I was overwhelmed by the thousands of times I had wanted to scream but didn't.

I'd seen it all – the bruises, the broken spirits, the fear etched onto faces like a permanent tattoo. Intimate Partner Violence. Familial Violence.

The clinical terms felt inadequate, a pathetic attempt to label the monstrous reality. But now, thanks to the Adverse Childhood Experiences study, I had a number.

Nine out of ten.

A score that explained the pulmonary embolisms, the panic attacks, the autoimmune disorder attacking my skin, Vitiligo. A score that predicted my body would betray me long before my spirit could heal. A score that carried consequences, indiscretions, extramarital affairs, and consequently, unplanned pregnancies.

A score that meant I wasn't crazy. I wasn't weak. I wasn't broken beyond repair. But even amid this realization, a score that only I had the power to understand, regulate, and navigate through the wreckage of my behaviors, largely influenced by my pre-conditions and trauma response.

I was a survivor of childhood trauma trying to live in an adult body that remembered everything my mind tried to forget.

The number didn't save me that day.

But it was the beginning of understanding.

And understanding, I would learn much later, is where healing begins.

NINE
The Legs Of Advocacy

Living with Jennifer and her son, brought me face to face with the woman who would introduce me to the criminal justice system as a professional and not as the daughter of an inmate trying to visit and bond her out.

Joyce Allen, a whirlwind of sharp suits and even sharper wit. Her business card, crisp and official, declared her position in the Major Crimes Division of the Miami Dade State Attorney's Office. Her words, though, were what truly struck me – a clear, concise explanation of the criminal justice system, followed by a surprisingly gentle push: "Apply," she'd said, a glint in her eye. "Transportation coordinator. Victim's advocate. You could do it."

In 1994, at the age of 22, I was a homeowner, a parent to a daughter, and embarking on my career in criminal justice.

At that time, Katherine Fernandez-Rundle served as the Miami-Dade State Attorney, a role in which she was widely respected and often regarded with reverence. Mrs. Fernandez-Rundle, known as Kathy among her staff, was the first Cuban American to assume this position in Miami and had succeeded Janet Reno, who had been appointed as the nation's first female U.S. Attorney General.

Kathy has held the office for over thirty years and continues to serve as the Miami-Dade State Attorney at the time of this writing.

Commuting to downtown Miami each day presented its challenges, but the privilege of working in this office and serving the vulnerable community I was assigned to work with was worth every mile.

I was thankful to be employed, but it was the position itself that truly made a difference.

Serving as the Victim Witness Coordinator at the Miami-Dade State Attorney's Office in 1994 proved to be an invaluable opportunity – one whose profound impact becomes increasingly evident when reflecting on its influence three decades later.

The environment was fast-paced, friendly, and intense. Coffee aromas filled the halls. Late nights and coworkers walking me to my car were common.

This office served as a vital center for justice, where survivors came to be heard, supported, and comforted in their grief. The attorneys lacked time for this, so I handled it.

Our unit managed all logistics for court-ordered victims and witnesses, including travel, meals, counseling, work notes, medical reimbursements, and sometimes childcare during testimony.

I witnessed colleagues who exhibited the impact of demanding workloads alongside their dedication to their duties. For instance, they worked extended hours to cover a murder trial due to a judge's late schedule and occasionally missed important family events because attorneys required additional time for depositions.

Additionally, there were occasions when less experienced attorneys, coping with the disappointment of an unsuccessful trial, treated us unprofessionally.

However, the attorneys also consistently demonstrated appreciation by taking us to lunch, presenting us with flowers, and offering sincere apologies when necessary.

Although the job was demanding and experiencing a trial loss could at times be discouraging, these attorneys remained deeply committed to their cases.

As advocates, we shared this dedication by diligently supporting the attorneys assigned to us – ensuring that we managed our caseload effectively and that every victim and witness listed for trial was located and prepared to testify in court when required.

Senior attorneys offered guidance and support to junior staff; they were both protective and committed to teaching them the importance of professional development.

They provided instructions to their assigned legal teams on effectively utilizing office staff to enhance case outcomes. A prosecutor's ability to present a well-prepared case in court –

regardless of the verdict – relies on having a competent and cohesive office team.

We were all well aware of this core principle within the office; therefore, we always got our flowers. We celebrated victories together, and sometimes we grieved losses together, sometimes in the courtrooms, with the families.

I spent seven years working with mentors in the Victim/Witness Unit who were and still are forces of nature.

Their dedication to creating innovative programs to help serve and protect victims of violent crimes was infectious, and their determination unshakeable.

I watched them craft grant proposals, attend meetings, writing furiously to capture ideas and bring the vision to fruition. These were abstract concepts that needed to be transformed into tangible programs.

I saw firsthand the impact of DART – Domestic Assistance Response Team – and its ability to reach out to survivors within 24 hours to offer relocation to shelters or financial assistance.

I was one of the first advocates to work with a program that has saved lives by providing rapid response to battered families, including men, women, children, and the elderly.

My last position with the office was with the Mobile Operations Victims Emergency Services, M.O.V.E.S. unit.

My caseload was a combination mixed with threads of suffering: stalking, sexual assault, domestic violence, the insidious creep of elder exploitation and homicide cases.

Faces flashed before my eyes – a young mother clutching a child, a stooped elderly man, the hollow-eyed gaze of a young man who spoke only Spanish.

The phone rang, sharp and insistent. "*Señora… por favor…*" The voice was barely a whisper. I braced myself.

This wasn't a 9-to-5 job. This was triage for the soul.

Sometimes it was the hospital's sterile scent of antiseptics, the dimmed light of the ICU hospital hallway, or the soft dignity of the forensic nurse.

I watched, my heart a lead weight, as the delicate process of evidence collection unfolded – a dance of precision, a grim ballet of trauma and hope.

My role – advocate, witness, protector – felt both immense and acutely fragile.

Later, the air turned to lead. A mother's heartbroken wail echoed in my ears as I delivered the news at 4:00 AM that her son was killed by a drunk driver while riding his motorcycle.

The paperwork for the Victim Compensation Fund blurred – funeral expenses, relocation, counseling… a cascade of costs born from violence.

This work gnawed at me.

It demanded everything: empathy, strength, and resilience honed by years of witnessing humanity's darkest moments. But in certain moments, in the occasional, hesitant smile of a survivor, I found something deeper than just relief: a profound and humbling sense of purpose.

The intersection of hope and despair? I knew it intimately. It was the very street I walked down every day. Not for me, but for others.

I was assigned one of the most difficult cases of my career when I was twenty-three years old.

A family shattered by a drunk driver's recklessness, barely surviving. The mother's voice, firm and unapologetic over the phone, still haunts me. "My boys," she whispered, her words trembling with anger, "They keep screaming, wondering if their dad is going to be ok."

I could almost see the two young faces, wide-eyed with terror, replaying the sickening crunch of metal, the sight of their father, an Army veteran, his face contorted in pain, his body crumpled against the twisted wreckage of the family car.

He'd just come home from the military, trading his fatigues for the quiet comfort of family. Now, his future, their future, lay in splintered pieces.

The impact had been on his side, the passenger side. I imagined the sheer force, the brutal physics that stole his ability to walk, to speak clearly, to be the provider he'd always been.

The doctor's notes spoke of severe brain trauma, a life sentence to a slow, agonizing recovery. Their home, once filled with laughter and the scent of home-cooked meals, was replaced by the generous, echoing silence of their sister's spare bedroom in a state far from Florida, a world away from the life they knew.

When I finally met them, their grief crowded the room. The mother's eyes, weary, held a deep fury. She didn't meet my gaze, her shoulders hunched as if bracing for another blow. The very mention of South Florida – the scene of the accident, the courthouse where they'd once felt so helpless – sent a tremor through her.

There was something else besides anger; it was deep disappointment in a system that seemed to have failed them. I saw it in the way she clenched her fists, the slight tremor in her jaw, the way she avoided my gaze, the exhaustion around her eyes. Her words weren't needed. Her pain was loud enough.

It wasn't enough to offer coping skills, to simply acknowledge their pain. No, this needed something more, something deeper.

So, I offered hope. Not empty platitudes, but the genuine promise of support, of assistance in navigating this labyrinthine legal process, of a chance, however small, to find some semblance of justice.

The exchange wasn't filled with detailed promises, just a delicate understanding, a connection forged in shared anguish and a spark of renewed determination.

In the end, Louisa, the mother, nodded, a fragile trust blooming in her eyes.

The flight tickets were booked, the hotel reservation made; a small step forward, a journey toward a future where perhaps, just perhaps, they could begin to heal.

The courtroom air was freezing after breaking a sweat in the hot and humid air of South Florida trying to make it to court on time.

I was barely out of my teens, a fledgling advocate, but something in my gut – a stubborn refusal to back down – kept my voice steady.

I spoke to the family, my words painting a picture not of despair, but of the stubborn, tenacious hope I knew bloomed even in the cracks of tragedy.

Miami shimmered under a relentless sun, but the family's faces were scarred with shadows.

I remember how that file anchored my hands as I navigated the convoluted system of Victim's Compensation. The slow, deliberate scratching of my pen on the forms as I said a prayer for the application to be approved and their medical bills paid.

The Victim Compensation Fund has been an important tool for every advocate who has had to navigate some of the tragic losses with a family due to a crime.

I completed the application on behalf of the family, and when the check arrived, I realized how important my role was: If I did my job, they would receive compensation that would immediately improve their quality of life. If I was lazy and didn't bother, they would not receive compensation – it was that simple.

That small victory fueled me.

Later, I watched as the father, his wheelchair a testament to his strength, rolled into their new home.

The resources obtained through the Victim Compensation Fund were enough to help them pay some medical bills. I followed up with a few calls and letters to help them restore their credit to help them qualify for a home of their own.

The work that I did with this family went far beyond the courtroom. To someone else it was four walls and a roof, but to them, it was the restoration of their dignity. The keys, cold and heavy in his hand, were the symbol of a future rebuilt.

Then came the Orlando trip.

I dialed the number to Disney and advocated for a family vacation for this family with two young sons. One call, a simple request, my voice as a conduit for their dreams.

The family received a beautiful, all-expenses-paid vacation. Another perfect victory on behalf of the kids in the fight for their happiness.

The photos from the trip arrived later; their laughter, bright and clear as the Florida sun, echoed the triumph of their resilience and the impact of an advocate doing their job.

Those young boys became fathers, college graduates, and one of them followed in his father's footsteps by wearing a military uniform, serving in the Army. The other son, in his lab coat, a scientist forging a new path. The father, Phillipe Arrieux, still providing, still nurturing, his spirit unbroken. He'd held onto his dignity, his family, his home, his life.

This was the soul of the whole thing, more than the 'advocacy' bit in a job description.

Thirty years later, seeing their success was a living testament, a vivid tapestry woven with hard work, hope, and the enduring power of the human spirit.

The Miami Herald article, the Neighbors Helping Neighbors – these organizations helped me help this family rebuild from the ground up. We wanted them to thrive instead of simply survive… and thrive they did.

The power of community support is the tangible results of believing in the impossible.

At the City of Miami Police Department, a young woman, her face blotchy and swollen, waited for me to take her sworn statement.

I felt drained, emotional, raw.

She recounted the events of the night before. Her voice, barely a whisper, caught in her throat as she described the brutal attack. I watched the tremor in her hand as she held a bottle of water.

Her eyes were full of tears as she asked me if she had to press charges.

My response was always the same: "No, you don't have to press charges – you just have to swear that you will tell me the truth, and I will photograph your injuries."

As long as I did my job correctly, collected all the necessary evidence, she didn't have to come to court.

But the day I met the victim, my job was to provide safety, collect evidence, and ensure that she understood that she did the right thing by calling the police and having him arrested.

After a difficult night with a victim at the crime scene, I would attend the bond hearing.

Once in the old courtroom at the Metro Justice Building, I would see the same fear radiating from her abuser.

Courtrooms that I became acquainted with the many times my mother was arrested, and then as a criminologist working for the State Attorney.

I would watch their small daughter, all of six years old, huddled against her mother, her thumb firmly in her mouth.

These were the daily snapshots of shattered lives.

Sometimes, in the delicate moments between cases, I would stand in those same hallways where I once stood as a teenager trying to bail out my mother. The fluorescent lights were the same. The worn linoleum tiles were the same. The smell of industrial cleaner mixed with fear and desperation – that was the same too.

But I was different.

That terrified seventeen-year-old girl who begged judges for treatment instead of release, who counted crumpled bills for bond money, who knew the Women's Detention Center visiting hours by heart – she had become the woman with the badge and the business card.

The woman who could help.

I saw myself in every victim I served.

In the young mother with bruises she tried to hide – I saw my mother's concealer-covered fingerprints.

In the woman who apologized for calling the police – I heard my own voice saying "sorry" after being violated.

In the children clinging to their mothers in courtrooms – I felt my own small hand reaching for safety that never came.

Every case was a chance to give someone what I had needed. What I had begged for. What no one had offered me.

The work was relentless.

Some nights I would drive home from a crime scene at 3 AM, still smelling the metallic tang of blood, still hearing a mother's wail, still feeling the intensity of a child's terrified stare.

I would pull into my driveway, sit in the car for long minutes, and try to remember how to be Josie the mother, Josie the wife, Josie the college student.

How to shed Josie the advocate who had just photographed a woman's broken nose, who had just held a rape survivor's hand during evidence collection, who had just explained to a six-year-old why Daddy couldn't come home.

But something was happening in those years at the State Attorney's Office.

With each family I helped rebuild, with each victim who found her voice, with each child who got to see their father roll into a new home despite his wheelchair – I was learning something crucial.

Systems could work. Support could heal. Community could restore what violence had destroyed.

One phone call to Disney could give two traumatized boys a week of childhood joy. One properly filed compensation form could mean the difference between a family losing everything or starting over. One advocate showing up, staying present, refusing to look away – it mattered.

I began to see the pattern.

Domestic violence wasn't just individual tragedy. It was epidemic. It was everywhere – in the courthouse hallways, in hospital emergency rooms, in police reports stacked on my desk, in the faces of children who learned too early what fear looks like.

And most people had no idea.

They thought it happened to other people. In other neighborhoods. To other families.

They didn't know that the woman at the grocery store had a broken rib under her sweater. That the man at church controlled every dollar his wife spent. That the couple down the street with the perfect lawn fought battles behind closed doors that left invisible scars.

The first seven years of this work. Of witnessing, documenting, advocating. Seven years of making a difference one case at a time while the epidemic raged on.

And somewhere in those courtrooms, in those hallways, in those hospital rooms and crime scenes, a vision was forming.

Not clear yet. Not fully formed. But growing.

A vision of something bigger than individual advocacy.

Something that could wake people up. Something that could reach beyond one victim, one family, one courtroom at a time.

I didn't know it yet, but I was preparing for a walk that would change everything.

All I needed was a spark.

A story that would ignite everything I had learned, everything I had witnessed, everything I had survived.

That tragic spark would come on September 26, 1999.

Her name was Gladys Ricart.

TEN

Between Vision And Walk

Before I could even catch my breath after the Destin vision, the annual 5K for the Domestic Violence Shelter flashed into my mind – the event was next Saturday. The words escaped before I could stop them, a ludicrous, desperate cry for attention and action: "Maybe I should run the 5K... in my wedding gown!"

The words left my lips initially as a gentle sign of commitment, only to be followed heavy with self-reproach. I wanted to crawl under the covers and disappear.

But I knew Adrian. That simple, understated "okay" wasn't dismissal. It was a quiet declaration of accountability, a secret promise that he would be there, holding me to my impulsive, wildly inappropriate plan. And he did.

The October air was hot and humid that Saturday morning. I stared at my reflection. My wedding dress, creamy ivory, only two years old and only worn once. The silk whispered against my skin, "What are you doing?" A discussion I refused to have with my dress.

I knew politicians, stern-faced detectives, colleagues whose opinions mattered – all of them would be watching. The whispers started in my head – It's too soon. They'll judge you. You'll lose your job. Who do you think you are? The words echoed, a relentless drumbeat of self-doubt. Then Adrian's hand was on my shoulder, his touch warm and reassuring.

It was the same dress I'd worn on April 25th, 1998, the day Adrian and I pledged our love, only two years ago. My daughters, oblivious to the emotional rollercoaster I was on, bounced excitedly, their energy a welcome distraction.

The drive to Bayfront Park blurred. I focused on the board I'd crafted, newspaper clippings and photos of Gladys's story forming a stark visual narrative.

At the registration table, the bustling energy of the crowd seemed to amplify my anxiety. Adrian helped me into the dress, the familiar weight suddenly feeling less like a burden, more like a symbol.

Lissette, my co-worker, her eyes brimming with unshed tears, approached. She'd seen the story in my office, read it, and absorbed it. "Josie," she said, "you are so brave." Relief washed over me as she gently took the board, freeing my hands.

My other colleagues nodded in support; I didn't need words to know they were on my side. The Miami Police Domestic Violence Detectives – the men who'd driven me to countless crime scenes, who'd witnessed the chilling aftermath of violence firsthand – stood guard along the route, their presence a reassuring bulwark against the inner turmoil. We shared a look of understanding of the shared trauma, the shared risk, the shared commitment.

Miami's thick and steamy air was my running mate as I ran my first 5K in my wedding gown. This was the signature event for the domestic violence movement in South Florida. Co-workers and law enforcement looked perplexed, their bodies stiff and somber as I ran past them filled with an endurance that only the stress hormone, cortisol, could fuel.

Every puzzled look, every negative or positive comment I heard as I tried to find a rhythm that my untrained body could sustain reminded me of Gladys. She was running through me. She was making sure that in the first year of her assassination, the world would start to prepare to feel the impact of her life.

The finish line was a blur of flashing cameras and outstretched microphones. The media, drawn by the story, swarmed. "No comment," I repeated mechanically, the words a practiced shield against the potential fallout. The rules were clear; silence was the safest option. The long shadow of Katherine Fernandez Rundle's office trailed me – every step, every breath, a calculated risk.

But even through the blur of my tears, I saw it – the startled expressions, the whispered comments, the cameras rising to capture this bizarre spectacle. A woman, alone, running in a wedding gown. The cameras didn't lie; this was a statement, whether I intended it or not. Crossing the finish line felt like a small victory, a gasp for breath in a world that held its breath.

Monday morning in the office, the congratulations felt laced with a strange mixture of awe and confusion. The questions, though, those were sharp. "You're going to leave your family for this?" A coworker's voice, sharp and accusing. I looked at her, feeling the sting. I swallowed. "Yes, I am," I managed to respond. "My kids have fathers. They'll be okay."

Another question, barbed and insistent. "But why?"

I met their gaze, letting the presence of my commitment settle on me. "Why not?" I finally said, my voice stronger now. "It's obvious. People blame victims. We need to change that. We need to educate everyone about the dangers of domestic violence. Don't you think?"

No response. That's when it hit me. My coworkers thought they were immune.

As I continued to plan and prepare, the snickers stung worse than outright negativity. "Forrest Gump," they'd call me, the condescending chuckle trying to hide the real intent behind it – to ridicule me.

Others warned, their voices laced with pity, that I was committing professional suicide. Every dismissive comment, although frustrating, informed me about the lack of knowledge and vision from many working in the field of domestic violence.

Yet a strange counterpoint played out. The local criticisms were drowned out by a chorus of national support – a wave of encouragement washing over the doubt. I pressed on, pushing past the familiar comfort of my routine.

I started to review the newsletters and brochures from the conference in Destin, Florida. A single article caught my eye: two young women cycling from California to Washington D.C. to raise awareness about sexual abuse. The words swam before me, but the image – the sheer audacity of their journey – sparked something. I raced home, my heart pounding, desperate to learn more.

I reached out to a 411 operator to ask for Nicole's number. I left a message for her and sent her an email. Within a few hours, we were on the phone.

Nicole Nadeau's voice, calm and reassuring, eased the fear that had gripped me. She understood. Not just the logistical challenges, but the raw, burning passion fueling my walk. It wasn't just advice she offered – it was a friendship forged in shared purpose, a sisterhood born in a single phone call. We talked for almost an hour.

Her insights on contacting agencies, crafting a media kit – it was practical, yet infused with an empathy that felt profoundly validating. That first call was a turning point. Nicole's guidance went beyond just about maps and permits; it also become about strategy, about belief. She helped me distill my purpose into a concise pitch, a fifteen-second elevator speech:

"Hi, my name is Josie Ashton. I am planning a walk from New Jersey to Miami in my wedding gown to honor a bride named Gladys Ricart who was killed on her wedding day by a jealous ex-boyfriend while her fiancé waited for her at the altar."

My words, sometimes met with stunned silence, other times with questions that poured forth like a torrent: "Did you know her?" "Why are you doing this?" "Are you raising money?" The incredulity in their voices – "You're leaving your family to walk cross-country in your wedding gown?" – was a testament to the audacity of the undertaking. But with each question, my resolve solidified. The journey, once a hazy dream, began to take tangible shape.

The more every piece fell into place, the more I needed to face the inevitable. I had to notify my job. My fingers hovered over the keyboard as I crafted the email. The words were a careful balancing act between hope and dread.

September 11, 2001.

The shrill ring of the phone sliced through the quiet. Adrian's mother. Her voice, a tremor of relief and exhaustion, painted a vivid picture: hours spent walking from downtown Manhattan to Queens, the city's arteries choked, the subway a lifeless thing. Judy, Adrian's sister, was with her. The phone became unreliable, but each call received was a small wave of connection in the rising tide of national grief.

Over the next 48 hours, we painstakingly accounted for family, one name, one reassuring voice, at a time. That week, the girls remained nestled at home, our small sanctuary shielded from the ever-present news broadcasts. The city, the country, felt like it was holding its breath.

My resignation from the State Attorney's Office, already submitted, felt insignificant compared to the world outside. My last day at work was already scheduled for September 20th, a date now overshadowed by the unimaginable events of the 11th.

Adrian and I had agreed to continue the walk, but a knot of uncertainty tightened in my chest. Would the New York organizations, the Ricart Family, even understand? They were grappling with another disaster of unimaginable scale, a collective trauma that threatened to overwhelm them all. But even in the midst of this national tragedy, my question to Adrian was, "are we still on?" his response, "we were never off."

Then came the call from Grace Perez, the cement that glued our movement. Her voice, usually bright, was tight with worry. "September twenty-sixth... the walk... Ridgefield to Flushing... after... after what happened..." The unspoken words were crystal clear between us. I heard the tremor in her voice, the underlying fear.

"The team's together, Grace," I said, my own voice steadier than I felt. "Shaken, yes, deeply affected... but we're moving forward. The walk is still on." The words felt brittle, even to my own ears, a fragile shield against the enormity of the situation. The date – September 26th, 2001 – felt impossibly close, a looming deadline in the face of unimaginable loss.

Grace called me back after our brief conversation the day before. "We're behind you, one hundred percent," she said, her voice still subdued but firm. "The Ricarts too. They're with us." Their support felt like a tangible thing.

"Unchanged," I'd told her. The words echoed in my mind, hollow now. Unchanged? Everything had changed. The world had changed. But the mission – Gladys's mission – that remained. Somehow, in the midst of national tragedy, walking for a bride murdered by her ex-boyfriend felt both more urgent and more fragile than ever.

The final weeks blurred into a frenzy of preparation. Phone calls. Emails. Planning routes. Confirming shelters. Packing and repacking. The wedding dress, carefully preserved, came out of storage. I held it up to the light, examining every seam, every detail. This dress – symbol of my marriage, symbol of Gladys's stolen future – would carry me 1,300 miles.

Adrian and I sat together in the evenings, poring over budgets, routes, shelter contacts. It wasn't about families or jobs or the looming threat of war – the things that should have consumed us. No, it was about our unbelievable promise: me, in my wedding dress, walking over 1,000 miles across a grieving nation.

I thought about the 5K race, just a year ago. How impossible it had seemed then to run 3.1 miles in a wedding gown. Now I was preparing to walk more than four hundred times that distance. The absurdity of it hit me in sudden moments – usually late at night when I couldn't sleep, my mind racing through logistics and fears.

What if my body gave out? What if shelters turned me away? What if people thought I was crazy? What if this entire mission – born from a spiritual vision in a Florida hotel room – was nothing more than my own trauma manifesting as delusion?

But then I'd see Gladys's face in my mind. Not from the news footage, but from the wedding photos I'd collected. Her smile. Her hope. Her son beside her. The future that was stolen from her on what should have been the happiest day of her life.

And I knew. Crazy or not, prepared or not, ready or not – I was walking.

Adrian and I drove to NYC with our girls in my two door Honda Civic. Mama Doreen had taken the time to cook for us and ensure that we were comfortable in her guest room.

September 25, 2001. The night before, Adrian kept the girls busy. I needed to be alone with my thoughts, alone with my fear, alone with God.

The room was quiet. Too quiet. I could hear my own heartbeat, feel the anxiety crawling up my spine. I pulled out the wedding dress one more time. Laid it across the bed. Stared at it.

Two years ago, I'd worn this dress to marry Adrian. Sixty guests. Ten tables. Rose petal invitations. A future full of promise.

Tomorrow, I'd wear this same dress to walk from a crime scene to a church. From death to what should have been abundant life. After that first day, a 1,300 miles journey from Ridgefield, New Jersey to Miami, Florida. From grief to... what? Justice? Awareness? Healing?

I didn't know.

I knelt beside the bed, my hands gripping the white fabric. And I prayed. Not the polished prayers of my childhood, not the careful words I'd learned from Mama. Just raw, honest pleading.

"I don't know if I can do this. I don't know if I'm strong enough. I don't know if this will matter. But You told me to walk, so I'm walking. Please... please open every door. Please protect my family. Please let Gladys's story change something. Please let this mean something."

The presence I'd felt in Destin didn't return. No swirling leaves. No voice like thunder. Just silence. Just me and the dress and the impossible task ahead.

But somehow, the silence was enough.

I had said yes in that Florida hotel room. The vision had been clear: Walk in your wedding dress, and change the headlines about Gladys Ricart. I'd run the 5K. I'd made the calls. I'd found Nicole. I'd survived September 11th and still said yes. I'd told my job, told my family, told the world.

Tomorrow morning, September 26, 2001 – exactly two years after Gladys was murdered – I would stand at the crime scene in Ridgefield, New Jersey, put on this wedding dress, and start walking.

1,300 miles.

In a wedding gown.

For a woman I'd never met.

For every woman who'd said no and was killed for it.

For every family devastated by domestic violence.

For the epidemic no one wanted to see.

I folded the dress carefully and set my alarm. Morning would come soon enough. And with it, the walk that would change everything.

ELEVEN
The Healing Tribe

Adrian and the girls assisted me in packing my two-door red Honda Civic with gear. We started driving toward New York City on September 21st, 2001, marking the beginning of our trip, which had changed significantly but continued as planned.

After a 12-hour drive we checked into a Hampton Inn off I-95. Adrian's hand, warm and gentle, rested on mine as we drifted to sleep, the hum of the highway a low thrum in the distance.

We woke up to the pale, pre-dawn light, the air crisp in North Carolina where we spent the night. The drive was long, a blur of passing fields and towns, culminating in the fiery sunset painting the New Jersey sky.

Even then, the distance couldn't mask it – a haze, a smudge of ochre and grey on the horizon. Smoke. The lingering, scary ghost of Ground Zero, twelve days past its tragic and fiery birth.

Each mile closer to New York City felt like a heavier weight on my chest, a lead apron and a face mask slowly suffocating my breath.

The vibrant greens and yellows of the countryside bled into the harsher grays and browns of urban sprawl.

My grip on Adrian's hand tightened. Across the car, the children chattered excitedly, unaware of the growing dread that coiled in my stomach. The Verrazano-Narrows Bridge was ahead of us, a steel giant against the darkening sky. As we ascended, the city spread before us like a wounded animal, its skyline scarred and broken.

The silence in the car was loaded with emotions, humid with tears, only the tires were showing any kind of enthusiasm. Adrian's hand had a solid, warm, and steady grip on mine. The kids' excited chatter felt miles away, a fragile bubble of joy in the face of looming despair.

On September 26, 2001, we gathered in front of Gladys Ricart's home, the place where she was murdered. It was 7:00 AM, and I was surrounded by an amazing group of individuals including Gladys's Family.

The core members of the coalition which was formed to support the family after the murder were also with me that morning. We stood at the crime scene where two years earlier horrendous chaos and confusion occurred.

As we held hands in a circle, we prayed before starting the first 1,300-mile Brides' Walk along the East Coast. I remember praying for a safe and meaningful walk, and for God's will to be done since I had very little idea of what I was about to get into.

Adrian was with me and our eyes met. I could feel the energy of the year we both invested expecting this moment. I could feel the energy of uncertainty and fear. But more than anything, I could feel that we were both exactly where we needed to be, doing exactly what we needed to do, without regrets. His love and confidence in this project brought me tremendous peace; I had the walk, and Adrian had our girls.

One step, and then another, and then many others after that. We began walking with a solemn demeanor, almost with mourning energy that had begun to transform over the past 22 years. What began as a sign of grief has evolved into a demonstration of faith, hope, thriving resiliency and empowerment.

On September 26th, 2001, only fifteen days after the September 11th terrorist attacks, we exited Ridgefield, New Jersey, located in Bergen County, and made our way to the George Washington Bridge in upper Manhattan.

We were not surprised when the Port Authority Police Department stopped us and explained that due to security issues, only four people were able to cross the bridge on foot. Our team quickly decided that Juan, Gladys's brother, and his wife would go with Adrian and me.

Crossing George Washington Bridge was extremely emotional. I looked at Adrian's face and realized that he grew up in New York and this was his first time back after the attacks. I paused to check on him and I could see so many emotions on his face. We held hands and discussed what this walk meant to us again.

We had these conversations before, but on September 26, 2001, walking on George Washington Bridge, the conversation took a very different turn for both of us.

As professionals, we wanted to raise awareness. We wanted to shift the conversation away from victim-blaming and toward education – toward helping communities understand what violence in the home really looks like and how it quietly destroys lives.

But as parents, the conversation felt different.

We felt it in our chests.

We worried about the world our children were inheriting. We worried about what they were being exposed to – the normalization of aggression, the celebration of dominance, the subtle ways power and control were woven into the fabric of society. It felt as if something sacred was unraveling.

On that bridge, Adrian and I stood side by side, but we were standing in two very different emotional landscapes. He was a New Yorker carrying the weight of September 11th in a way that is carved into the bones of that city. I was a survivor carrying September 26th – the day Gladys Ricart was murdered on her wedding day – in my nervous system.

Different dates. Different scales. Different contexts.

And yet, both left families shattered.

Both altered legacies.

Both were born from the same human impulse: the need to dominate, to control, to exert power over another life.

On September 26, 1999, one family's world was irreversibly transformed. On September 11, 2001, our nation's sense of safety was fractured in a way that would redefine a generation.

The magnitude was not the same.

But the root – violence in the name of power – was.

And standing there, we both understood something devastating: whether in a home or on a national stage, when violence is justified by control, everyone loses something that cannot be fully restored.

Our conversation was interrupted by enthusiastic drivers, blowing their horns assuming that Adrian and I were on our way to get married. Drivers were waving at us, taking pictures, and wishing us good luck. They had no idea that our walk was about a bride killed by a jealous ex-boyfriend.

They did not know that the killer was about to face trial and blame his victim for his actions. But worst of all, they certainly did not know that people die daily, even when they are not in an abusive relationship, because of the effects caused by domestic violence.

Adrian and I decided that we wanted to change that by doing everything possible even after the walk, to educate, empower, and help people heal.

Our walk on September 26, 2001, lasted over 12 hours. We made a few stops to talk to the media, use the restroom, and have lunch. The New York team wanted to make sure that the route included Washington Heights, Spanish Harlem, and the Bronx, areas deeply affected by domestic violence.

We arrived at the Church on the Hill a little after 7 PM. The Church in Flushing, New York, was the church Gladys chose to marry her fiancé, James Preston. We were welcomed by the media, and we had to be firm when explaining to the media that this event was for the family.

As important as the media has been and continues to be for us to get our message across, I personally wanted the family to have a space to grieve without the media photographing every tear and emotion. This evening needed to be private.

The family never made it to church on September 26, 1999, and this was their first time setting foot in the venue where their loving Gladys and her fiancé chose to be married, and I refused for that moment to be taken away from them by cameras and questions.

The Pastor that was going to marry the couple held a beautiful ceremony in which he shared some of his experiences on that very tragic day. Her niece, Lethy Liriano, who was next to Gladys when she was shot and killed. She was supposed to sing "A Ribbon in the Sky" by Stevie Wonder the day of the wedding, and on September 26, 2001, she sang the song in her honor.

The New York Team, formed from key organizations in Upper Manhattan, helping the Ricart family, was able to discuss their commitment to the family, and I had an opportunity to discuss the concept and the vision of walking 1,300 miles in my wedding gown for the next 72 days. On this night we formed our Healing Tribe!

It was that night that we realized that the Ricart Family was mourning and grieving but so was the Dominican community as well as the community at large. This is the night that we decided to bond and heal together. The night ended with emotional hugs and handshakes signifying solidarity and commitment.

September 27th, 2001, I had to face my own fears. I was determined and had goals laid out to complete this journey, but I truly did not know how I was going to do it other than with faith and with the pain I was carrying.

I helped Adrian and the girls get ready to return back home to a life without me for the next few months. I was overwhelmed with sadness and terrified with fear. Not having Adrian by my side was nerve-wracking, not having my girls, left me with a profound feeling of emptiness and lack of joy.

I drove them to the train station and managed to say goodbye without crying. But once I stepped into my car and drove to what was meant to be my starting point, I began to weep.

Every single doubt and negative thought began to flood my mind like a tsunami. I drove for hours and ended up pulling over into a market parking lot. I decided to get something to eat and while I was getting ready to pay, I looked at the newspaper stand.

I remembered that a reporter interviewed me, and I bought a newspaper with not much hope of seeing the story, after all, my negative voices just spent hours talking to me about what a stupid idea this was. But there it was, a very well-written article by a reporter that had been following the case with pictures and even a few encouraging words.

I was no longer thirsty or hungry, I put my iced tea in the car holder and called Adrian to share the article. He was happy to hear from me and shared how proud he was of me and the work I was doing. Yet, the moment we hung up the phone, I started crying again. Those voices were so loud and convincing:

"You think one newspaper article is important? People will not even read it. Get a hold of yourself, stop dreaming!"

I was emotionally and physically exhausted. I went through my phone looking for someone to call. One of my aunt's name came up; she lived in Newark and worked as a manager at one of the high-end chain hotels.

As soon as she heard my voice, she gave me her address and told me to meet her at the restaurant inside the hotel. When I arrived, she just hugged me and let me cry. She then ordered dinner and had a room ready for me to rest.

I stayed alone at the hotel that night. My aunt knew I needed to be alone. I was emotionally naked and vulnerable. I was not the strong woman and inspiring activist from the day before.

On September 27, 2001, I was the confused nine-year-old who was sexually abused; the young teen that was neglected; and the young adult that was abused by her first boyfriend during her senior year of high school. I had not seen or felt those wounds in a while, but they all started surfacing that day.

My desire to bring healing to others began revealing my own open wounds from childhood abuse, exposing my pain, and ultimately connecting me with my shame. Not a good feeling in the middle of doing something of this caliber. It was during the very beginning of the walk that all my childhood memories began to overwhelm my spirit.

I was not expecting that. In my mind, I didn't have trauma. I was aware of having experienced sexual abuse and domestic violence, but these memories and persistent fear and anxiety were foreign to me.

As my walk progressed and I had more interactions with survivors, I found myself numbing my emotions. I had no time to process any negative feelings because each day was too important for the work I was doing.

The first day was over. Twelve hours of walking. A ceremony at the church where Gladys never made it. A Healing Tribe formed. And then – the collapse.

I had 1,288 miles left to walk.

And I had just discovered that the walk wasn't only for Gladys. It was for the nine-year-old girl inside me who had never been allowed to weep.

TWELVE
Trenton To Verdict

Womenspace in Trenton, New Jersey, was the first shelter to welcome me. Susan Switlik, the Executive Director at the time, offered immediate warmth. The building was a beautiful brick structure nestled among ancient, sprawling trees.

The aroma of freshly brewed coffee hit me first, followed by the sight of a plate loaded with warm muffins. Later, a bag overflowing with granola bars and fruit – snacks for the road ahead – was pressed into my hands.

Her smile, though, was the most comforting. It held a depth of understanding that transcended words. She showed me to a small but clean room in the shelter – a sanctuary within a sanctuary – and her voice, calm and reassuring, chased away the shadows of doubt. "You're going to be okay," she said, and it felt like a promise whispered into the heart of my fear.

The next day unfolded in a flurry of activity. Susan and I sat at a worn wooden table, scattering papers between us. The blank page of my planning document seemed less daunting with her by my side.

Each suggestion – calling shelters proactively, crafting a press release – felt like a small victory in the battle against inertia. The heaviness of unanswered letters, a cold reminder of previous failures, lightened as we strategized, possibilities spreading before us like an unfolding map.

Finding safe walking routes became a shared quest. We scrolled through maps, marking potential paths: the safety of a park, the energy of a main street, the gravitas of a landmark.

Susan's instructions on trusting my instincts, on recognizing and responding to subtle shifts in my environment, were less like lessons and more like the imparting of a secret code, empowering me to navigate the unknown. Her words resonated: "Don't second-guess yourself. Your safety is paramount."

Leaving Womenspace, the brick building seemed to hold a piece of my heart. The trees whispered good luck. My feet ached, swollen from the first tentative steps of my journey, but the ache was overshadowed by a surge of empowerment. The initial uncertainty had been replaced by a powerful sense of self – a certainty that I could complete this walk. I could.

I continued to walk in public places, logging my miles, trying not to be distracted by intrusive negative thoughts. Susan's wisdom made me feel safe and calm. The last few days had been so lonely, but spending time with the clients in the shelter was the perfect way to recharge my energy.

From time to time, I would think about how some men had taken advantage of me, and the absence of nurturing female figures in my youth. Trust felt like a distant, unreachable concept.

But then, these women appeared – their hands, not just metaphorically, but literally, reaching out. One slipped me a twenty, another offered a listening ear that felt like a soft pillow for me to rest my head; a third, a prayer whispered under the dark of night. Their generosity was a soothing cream to my wounded spirit; it nourished my soul.

Before, I had often perceived the women leaders who entered my life through work or school as a threat. I was cautious, defensive, a shield forged in fear. But out on that road, with only their unwavering support, my armor split open. I felt God's grace, not in a booming voice, but in the gentle pressure of their presence, coaxing me into a humility I hadn't known I craved, and an assertiveness I hadn't dared to claim.

I left Trenton stronger, with a new sense of dignity and resolve. They helped me believe in the importance of the mission and the meaning of my voice. They straightened my walk, soothed my pain with their touch, and helped me believe that the rest of the journey was possible, no matter how uncertain it might seem.

Levittown, PA, stood in a haze of aching feet and mounting dread. Sixteen miles – a victory for a cold, soggy day – felt like a cruel joke when I stumbled back into the cheap hotel room.

The panic hit like a physical blow. My body shook, a ragged symphony of sobs and choked gasps. The 22-mile goal, a beacon just moments ago, now loomed as an impossible mountain, my deadline a guillotine's blade.

Florida, Adrian, the girls – they felt a million miles away, unreachable.

The room spun. Each breath felt like a struggle. Defeat tasted like failure in my mouth. The goal was 22 miles, not 16. Every day I missed my goal would delay my arrival. The more I analyzed the journey, the harder it was for me to breathe.

I called Adrian, his voice a lighthouse in the dark ocean of my despair. I heard the raw vulnerability across the phone line as he recounted his own post-law school odyssey – the desolate apartment, the gnawing loneliness, the fear that clung to him like a shadow. He didn't minimize my pain; instead, he mirrored it, his words a quiet affirmation of my experience.

"It's normal," he said, his voice calm, steady. "This too will pass." His words were a tangible thing, a hand reaching through the darkness. "You're safe," he repeated, the simple statement washing over me like a tide of relief. "You can come home."

The memory of those strange, silent towns, the phantom echo of the terrorist attacks a month before, the fear that had gripped me then, loosened its hold. My American pride, fractured by the recent blow to my US citizenship, blossomed anew. The panic subsided, replaced by a some deep strength strength, a rediscovery of my own power, and my country's power.

The rest of the walk was hard, but the tremors of those initial panic attacks never returned. Yes, America was bruised and battered and still in shock by the collective trauma we experienced on September 11, 2001. Many of the women I met in those shelters still had visible injuries as a result of the terror they experienced in their own homes. I was far removed from my own experience of teen dating violence and child abuse and neglect, but I continued to be deeply wounded.

That day I learned that we don't remain stagnant in our pain and fear. We move, we walk, we push, hard, often, forward.

October 1st, 2001. Domestic Violence Awareness Month. Hope had flared bright, promising speaking engagements, public awareness events.

The steering wheel felt slick with sweat as I navigated the Philadelphia streets, the city a concrete jungle closing in. Ten miles later, my shoes were dragging, each step a protest. Three shelter crisis workers' voices, three refusals – uninterested, too busy, too full to host me or entertain my work.

Then, a crack of light: Bel Air, Maryland. I asked for a week's stay to catch up on my miles and not worry about where to sleep. The shelter director said yes, and a wave of pure, unadulterated relief washed over me; a sob escaped before I could stop it.

October 2nd, 2001. The crisp Maryland air held a different chill. I reached out to the New York tribe, each ring raising my level of anxiety as I tried to find out the status of the murder trial scheduled for that week. The words tumbled out as an office staff provided details about the week ahead – jury selection.

What!? Really!? I was certain that the 9/11 attacks were going to postpone the trial. I was wrong. Jury selection for the criminal trial of Agustin Garcia in the murder of Gladys Ricart began October 2, 2001, at the Bergen County Courthouse.

The burden on my shoulders was replaced by a surge of purpose so potent it fueled my legs for nine more hours of relentless walking that day. Back at the shelter, a hush fell as I entered. I could feel their eyes on my feet – two swollen, angry things, purpled and misshapen.

Before I could even sit, two women were scrambling for a bucket of ice, another fumbling with a basin. The sting of the ice was immediate, excruciating, but it was quickly replaced by dull numbness. And then, laughter.

The kind of raw, cathartic laughter that comes from shared pain, from a recognition of the absurdity of it all, the way women bond over shared fury. That evening, the common area at the safe house was transformed with the chaotic energy of children – their shrieks and giggles, unaware of some of the dangers they were facing, allowed for some of us to watch in awe at the innocence of their resilience.

Later, as the little ones slept, the women sat with me in the living room as we shared stories, not painful stories, but stories of hope, new beginnings, and transformation. I used the same question my school counselor asked me when I was 17 years old and walked into her office with a black eye. "Tell me about your dreams."

They did. We circled, sharing our dreams, our gratitude, our fragile hopes. Each whispered confession of what seemed an impossible dream, each shared tears, solidifying my commitment to continue the walk.

We shouldn't be afraid to dream or ashamed to envision a future free of violence. Survival, just like day-to-day living, requires us to fully live, to contemplate tomorrow being a better day. Once fear and shame interrupt our ability to dream and conceive a better tomorrow, we cease to live and start to simply exist.

The weeks blurred. More shelters, more miles, more women's stories layering onto mine. I flew home to Miami for a weekend with Adrian and the girls, a brief respite before returning to the walk.

Evenings with Adrian a shared exhale. The soft lamplight illuminated the serious lines of his face as we pored over budgets, job postings, and the looming end of my walk – a culmination, not a finish line.

The weekend was too short. Monday morning, Adrian kissed me goodbye several times as he got ready for work. I took more time than usual to get the girls ready for school, giving them tons of kisses as I brushed their hair. I was ready to get in the cab to head to the airport, back to Norfolk, VA, when my cell phone rang.

Monday, October 22, 2001.

My fingers fumbled; it was a New York phone number. The team was calling me for the first time since jury selection started. I answered, "Hello," and all I heard were the words, "guilty as charged."

The world stopped for a few seconds. I didn't respond, couldn't respond, because I wasn't even holding my breath. My intentions were never to walk during the trial. I really thought the trial was going to be postponed in the wake of 9/11, but it wasn't. And here we were: guilty as charged.

I was usually in the courtroom when I heard a court clerk read the verdict, but this Monday, receiving the news over the phone, it felt different, meaningless, void of any power. For Gladys was dead, and her family was still suffering.

Augustin Garcia killed Gladys Ricart in front of her entire family on September 26, 1999. He was charged with first-degree murder, but the prosecution was concerned that the jury might find him guilty of manslaughter, a much lesser charge. That was one of the fears haunting me since his legal team suggested the Crime of Passion defense.

The thought of this man killing this beautiful bride and walking out of prison by using the "crime of passion" defense was an insult. A defense designed on the idea that his love for her was so passionate and overwhelming that it caused him to kill her was not only absurd but a threat to every person who would choose to end a relationship and move on. A lesser charge would diminish justice and threaten safety.

But no. First-degree murder.

The muffled roar of celebratory shouts in the background intensified. I joined in, but the sound of joyous cries only amplified the raw wound of Gladys's absence and all the other families I met daily, trying to hide from a fate like hers. Tears streamed down my face as the taxi drove me to the airport.

Justice doesn't bring healing.

But it was a start. And I still had 800 miles left to walk.

THIRTEEN
Nicole's Friendship

Nicole's embrace was warm and welcoming – a much-needed familiar stranger whose presence was incredibly soothing and reassuring. Howard, looking at us with joy in his eyes, pulled out a chair and joined us in laughter and conversation.

Their Washington, DC, apartment, nicely decorated with scattered art, Asian artifacts, and a bookshelf filled with various titles next to a cozy sofa, felt instantly welcoming. Nicole's eyes, though bright, held a shadowed depth.

I didn't know her story but after almost three decades of friendship, her book, once she decides to write it, is a substantial compilation of perseverance, sacrifices, and live-out-loud attitude in a world that can easily be offended with noise. My dear Nicole laughs with gusto. I love watching her life unfold and her grace facing new challenges.

She understood the painful ache in my chest, the exhaustion that went beyond physical fatigue, the heaviness of unspoken trauma that clung to me, before I did.

Laughter would bubble up between us, unexpected and joyous. Even when the tears that followed – silent at first, then released in a shared wave of emotion, our conversations would end with an irreverent feeling of joy punctuated by laughter. Our joy, her joy, is irreverent even today. She refuses to succumb to defeat and sadness, she wakes up every day asking the world, "What you got for me today, bring it!!!"

That night, the first time we met, high-fives echoed in the cozy space, a pact forged between two weary warriors.

The next morning, with Howard's guidance, I started an eight-mile journey to the White House. The miles guided me through monuments and bustling streets. I called my podiatrist in Florida for a quick phone consultation before meeting Judith, the Executive Director, for one of the shelters in DC.

Judith, a woman with both strength and compassion, met me for lunch at a small cafe. Her gaze, sharp and assessing, lingered a moment too long as I recounted my journey. Then came a decisive shake of her head. No shelter.

Instead, a warm hand on my arm provided firm yet gentle guidance toward a car – her own car – taking me to a home filled with the comforting scent of rice and peas and the low murmur of voices from a cozy kitchen where a kind, smiling man, her husband, waited for us to have dinner.

Words failed me then, swallowed by the unexpected kindness, the simple act of radical empathy that left me breathless.

The soles of my feet screamed constantly after solid days of walking without my shoe inserts, which I'd misplaced despite my podiatrist's strong recommendation not to go without them. My wallet felt the pinch too – cell phone minutes dribbled away like sand, gas prices threatening our dwindling savings, and even cheap motel coffee seemed a luxury.

The desperation to avoid hotel costs became a frantic hunt. Every night I had a place to sleep without needing to pay was a blessing.

A distant ray of light appeared on the horizon: Lynchburg, Virginia. A map showed it as a far western speck, a world away from where I was, but I needed their support, a place to stay, and survivors to fuel my spirit.

The YWCA, having seen my story on the local news, invited me to their vigil. Relief washed over me like a warm wave. Their welcome was astonishing: a full body massage and a night in a hotel room.

"A full body massage? I'd never had one," the thought of it made my body panic, immediately. Their offer, a luxurious treat, felt almost threatening, even after weeks of aching muscles and the constant, underlying tension of my journey.

Naked under the sheet, I felt my muscles tense up, each touch a jolt of unexpected sensation. I mumbled something about feeling awkward, my voice barely a whisper. The therapist's hands, though, were steady and reassuring, her touch surprisingly gentle. Together, we adjusted the draping and found positions that eased my discomfort.

But even with the accommodation, my body fought back – the stiffness, the involuntary resistance, was palpable.

I could feel her hands hovering, sensing my inability to relax, and I knew my face must be a mask of strained anxiety. The final touch was a release – a slow exhale of tension I hadn't even realized I was holding. My body, unused to the simple comfort of safe touch, had exposed me.

That experience changed me. Four times a year, at least, I schedule a massage now – a deliberate act of self-care, a conscious effort to teach my body to relax under gentle, non-sexual touch. It's become a crucial part of my healing, a gentle reminder that safe touch can be a calm and soothing experience, not a threat.

I drove to Virginia Beach, which was a completely different world. A gentle sea breeze, carrying the scent of salt and sun-warmed sand, met me as I entered the city. Stella's house – a cheerful and safe haven – welcomed me with a warm home meal, and tea, sweetened and spiced.

Stella's laughter echoed through the kitchen as she poured out generous portions of whatever deliciousness she'd conjured. The clinking of forks and the murmur of conversation created a comforting soundtrack to my days at her house. Ten to twelve miles each way – that's what it took to reach the ocean. Day after day, I walked, the sun painting the sky with blazing hues as I began my journey and painting it with softer pastels as I returned, exhausted but strangely exhilarated. Those twelve to thirteen hours were a reclamation project, a rebuilding of the time stolen by doubt and fear. And yes, I took my time.

But that first day... The vast, unfamiliar expanse of Virginia Beach, the looming presence of the Naval Air Station – it was a baptism by jet engine.

Herbie Hancock's smooth jazz, piped into my ears, did little to muffle the earth-shaking rumble that vibrated through my very bones. The ground itself seemed to shudder beneath the roar of the Super Hornets, each pass a guttural shriek overhead.

My heart hammered. The memory of everything surged back – a crushing flood of fear and anxiety. I was certain, absolutely certain, that the war had started or we were under attack, again.

I bolted for the nearest gas station, my breath irregular, my wedding gown – yes, the wedding gown! – swirling around my ankles. My panicked words spilled out in a breathless rush: "Why are there fighter jets? Are we under attack again? Is the war starting?"

The attendant, initially amused by my appearance, saw the genuine terror in my eyes. The sarcastic smile vanished. He stepped from behind the counter, his voice calm but firm: "No, everything's okay. We have a naval base. Military exercises. It's normal here."

My jaw dropped. Fighter jets? Over this quaint town? "Normal?" I echoed, my voice a breathless squeak. The shop assistant's sarcastic smile returned to his face, and it felt like a physical slap.

A few seconds stretched into an eternity as my brain rebooted. By then, the store was filling with customers. I could feel their eyes on me – a bride, white dress shimmering, face crumpled with bewildered distress, babbling to a smirking clerk.

Heat flooded my cheeks as I mumbled a thank you and practically fled, the image of their curious stares burning into my memory. Virginia Beach, a coastal pocket that felt quaint to me at the time, but it was anything but small – jets thundered overhead and the Atlantic carried more than tourists; it carried fleets.

Why hadn't Adrian's family given me a heads-up? That night, I unleashed my fury. Stella, Adrian's aunt, her husband, her son – their amusement was a thin veil over their unconcern. They shook their heads, smiling thinly. "Just as weird as you walking around in a wedding gown," they chirped.

I guess we were even. Then we slept.

The sound of the jets became a friendly reminder that our country was ready to defend our nation and go after those who dared attack us on September 11th. I woke up every morning looking forward to listening to the engines – the vibration became my favorite soundtrack to my days.

The roar of engines was a prelude to dipping my feet in the chilly Atlantic, the cold seeping into my busy toes as I swapped sneakers for bare feet. It was my perfect ritual, a refreshing break before heading back to the important intimacy of my room. I fell hard for Virginia Beach – its rhythm, its sea-washed air becoming a part of me.

☙

Emails and calls began flooding my inbox – invitations to events, speaking engagements. A call from a shelter in Beaufort, South Carolina, caught my attention.

The promise of food, shelter, and the chance to continue my mission swayed me. I drove seven hours, the miles unwinding before me as I headed south. The shelter emerged from the darkness – a modern, pristine building stark against the night sky.

A lone resident greeted me, her eyes cautious as she offered a sandwich and tomato soup. As we ate, I felt the unspoken question: Who are you? I sensed suspicion, perhaps even a fleeting thought that I was a woman escaping abuse. Introducing myself and explaining my journey felt insignificant compared to what she may be experiencing.

The moment I spoke of my walk, the dynamic between us shifted – a subtle change, but palpable, nonetheless. That shared experience of vulnerability never materialized. Her walls were thick and tall, impenetrable, we remained with unspoken understanding and mutual strangeness.

I continued to watch her move with grace and dignity as she walked me through the building. The lamps and fluorescent lights reflected off her skin, emphasizing her tense muscles. She moved with the same effortless grace as Michelle Obama – a younger, perhaps slightly more athletic version – her posture straight, her stride confident. She never once mentioned her own experiences, and somehow, her composure was enough.

Instead, she showed me the shelter, pointing out the fire exits and making sure the blankets were clean and to my liking before I settled in.

Fayetteville, NC, shimmered under a Carolina sun. The Arrieux family had invited me to stay with them for a week, which was a welcome relief for me to focus on logging miles and engaging the local news station.

I finally arrived at the Arrieux family home. Louisa's smile was as welcoming as the meal she had prepared for me. Jacque and Andreas, in their old teens, greeted me with shy grins, their eyes reflecting the easy camaraderie between them and their father, Philip. The dogs, two boisterous gorgeous beasts, free to greet me, their joyful barks a welcome chorus, music to my ears. Philip, from his wheelchair, greeted me with a warm smile and a hearty hug.

Later, the boys helped Louisa clear the table, their movements fluid and effortless. A shared laugh, a playful shove, a tender touch on their father's shoulder – their bond was beautiful. My heart was overwhelmed to see how they were thriving in North Carolina, after the tragedy in Florida.

Watching them interact in their home was such an honor. I had never witnessed that kind of love and familial strength. Spending time with them that evening reminded me of my girls. I went to bed feeling warmth spread through me, deeper than the delicious food, warmer than the fireplace. The guest room she prepared for me was a piece of heaven. A cozy sanctuary where I felt safe and welcome.

Wilmington, NC. The local shelter was one of the first who offered to host me before I left Florida. My inbox, usually a battlefield of unanswered pleas, had yielded a victory – a confirmation email from their local shelter, some hope in a sea of rejection.

But that hope was about to be dashed as I pulled into the city and entered the administrative offices. I never got to see their shelter or meet their clients. The cheerful representative's smile felt strained as she delivered the news: my promised two-night stay was cut to one.

My carefully planned chili cook-off participation, reduced to a token gesture. Then came the final blow: wearing my wedding gown was "too risky," a suggestion of impending harassment that left a bitter taste in my mouth. Something was wrong, terribly wrong, and I didn't know what.

The Bed & Breakfast, though lovely – a haven of lace curtains and antique furniture – couldn't mask the disquiet within. The owner, a kind man with warm eyes, couldn't soothe the growing unease. I stared at my reflection, the wedding gown hanging limply in the closet.

The local reporter asked me to get ready for photos and an interview within an hour. I was exhausted, but I knew how important the media was to spread the word about escaping abuse and sharing information about local shelters. Getting ready felt like dressing for a firing squad.

The reporter, a man with eyes that seemed to pierce through me, sat across from me on the plush velvet sofa. The living room, once a beautiful space, felt like a cage. Each question felt like an accusation, each click of his photographer's camera a hammer blow.

His gaze, scrutinizing and unforgiving, shrunk me down to an insignificant speck. Yet, a stubborn ember of defiance burned within. I answered his questions, my voice steady, if slightly trembling, meeting his gaze head-on.

The next morning, my gown looked sad on its hanger, a rebuke to the unexpected instructions I'd received. Instead, I opted for jeans and a simple sweater. The park was still mostly empty, the dew clinging to the grass. I started walking to log in miles and take advantage of the time I had.

Then I saw him – the reporter, a familiar figure driving by the park. His eyes, sharp and inquisitive, followed my every move. I offered a small, tight-lipped wave, a gesture that felt more like a challenge than a greeting. He made no attempt to disguise his pursuit, instead accelerating his pace towards the park's exit before quickly driving away in his vehicle.

The event loomed – a heavy, unavoidable shadow – as I approached the park. The stiff silk of my dress, now clutched in my arms like a shield, felt strangely inappropriate. Of course I had the dress; I was not attending the event without the dress. And then she was there, the shelter representative, her face a mask of practiced neutrality. She avoided my gaze, her words clipped and devoid of warmth, a staccato burst of cancellation, of irrelevance.

My feet moved before I could fully process her words. I pursued her, the heel of my sneakers sinking on the wet grass. Another person intercepted her first, their conversation a muffled blur. Seizing the opportunity, I cut in, my voice sharp and controlled, "Did you say you don't need me to speak today?"

The confirmation, a single, chilling word: "Yes." A curt nod, a curt "thank you," and I walked away, my wedding gown swinging lifelessly in my arms.

My head started throbbing. I dialed the reporter's number. My voice, shaky and annoyed, recounted the events: the hushed whispers, the pointed glances, the abrupt dismissal. He listened, his silence making me uncomfortable.

Then, almost indifferent, he replied, "Welcome to Wilmington." His words, delivered with a tone of cynicism, almost rehearsed, as if he had been waiting for the right moment to share his sarcastic welcome, dripping with unspoken meaning. The barely-concealed sneer I imagined on his face burned hotter than any accusation.

I returned to the Bed & Breakfast to pack my suitcase. I needed to get out of the town who rejected me, my work, and tried to hush my voice the minute they saw the color of my skin.

The drive to Myrtle Beach felt more like a runaway attempt, even though nobody was chasing me. My tears blurred the highway signs, and I was having a difficult time controlling my emotions. This wasn't the familiar sting of prejudice; this was something colder, more insidious – the shame of being silenced, not only for who I was, but by the organization that claimed to represent me.

I checked in to a dingy Motel 8 room which felt unsafe, but it was the only place I could afford on the strip. I called home after I checked in and Adrian's voice sounded worried. I tried to explain what happened, and what I understood happened.

The raw humiliation stuck in my throat as I spoke about the incident. "Rejected...because I'm Black?" The words finally escaped my lips. That night, sleep was a battlefield, a restless wrestling match with tears and prayers.

Once I arrived at the shelter, the staff, a group of amazing women with a few strong men, I was welcomed with faces full of kindness. I was allowed to stay for a week. They sent a press release, and Gladys's story, raw and vulnerable, unfolded on the evening news – two channels, their bright lights illuminating the stark reality of many families' living in violent environments. The local paper's headline also covered the story.

Every news story provided the community with the local resources to escape the violence. I started to feel strong and confident again. My walk was steady. I walked the Myrtle Beach streets, the cloud of homelessness and rejection lifted, each step a soft victory. A profound peace settled over me, the ocean salt gentle on my fractured spirit.

There were still hundreds of miles ahead. But for the first time in weeks, I believed I could walk them all.

FOURTEEN
The Movement Grows

December 6, 2001. The walk was over.

Seventy-two days. Thirteen hundred miles. Countless shelters, vigils, stories. I stood at the main entrance to the Florida International University in North Miami, the Atlantic behind me, my wedding gown stained brown and gray, the hem in tatters. Adrian and the girls were waiting. The Alpha phi Sigma Healing Tribe had gathered one last time to greet me. And as I took off the dress for what I thought might be the final time, I felt both relief and loss.

The walk, the full-time internship that had helped me accomplish this monumental effort was over. But the movement was just beginning.

In 2002, I graduated with my Bachelor's degree in Criminal Justice.

I started working at the Florida Attorney General's office under General Butterworth, a man whose presence filled the room with authority, his gaze holding the countless stories. I helped families navigate the aftermath of violence, the complex criminal justice system, while guiding their trembling hands through the labyrinth of crime compensation forms after a homicide or catastrophic injury.

I stood before rooms of seasoned officers and officers in training, my words shaping their understanding of compassion. I assisted families obtain funds for crime scene cleanup. Attended funerals, events, conferences, traveled, a lot.

As the grant season ended, I became the steady hand offering guidance and reassurance to local agencies that needed technical assistance navigating through grant requirements, victim services and certifications.

General Butterworth had entrusted me with this vital work. He spoke with a voice that resonated with a deep, unyielding commitment to the vulnerable survivors of trauma. I was honored to work under him.

That October morning in 2002, Biscayne Boulevard vibrated with hope and action. The same landmark that hosted me in 2000, when I wore my dress for the first time to run a 5K, now throbbed with a different kind of energy. The Domestic Violence Coalition decided to host the first Miami-Dade Brides' March at Bayfront Park.

Representatives from the Miami-Dade State Attorney's Office mingled with the earnest faces of the U.S. Attorney's Office. Across the park, a cluster of individuals from Safespace Shelter and the

Safespace Foundation, their voices carrying a defiant conviction. Staff from The Advocate Program and the Miami-Dade Domestic Violence Court stood shoulder-to-shoulder, their shared experience a palpable force. The Mayor of the City of Miami, several commissioners and the county manager were also in attendance.

Across the manicured lawns of Bayside, uniformed officers from the City of Miami Police Department on horses, their polished badges reflecting the morning light, joined their Miami-Dade counterparts, the Opalocka Police Department, North Miami Police Department, Miami Beach Police Department, and North Miami Beach Police Department – each a physical manifestation of their commitment that ran deeper than protocol.

The event embodied and amplified the collective force of prosecutors, law enforcement, and advocates as a living representation of community forged in action, forming yet another healing tribe.

As the marches began to multiply across cities, something inside me was multiplying too.

It was a sense that no matter how much I accomplished, it would never be enough to fill the hollow space childhood had carved out.

I didn't have words for it yet. I just kept moving, kept building, kept putting on the wedding gown and pretending it wasn't getting harder to do each time.

By 2004, two years after the walk, I stood in the Safespace Foundation boardroom – the same room where I'd pitched the walk to skeptical faces, the same room where someone asked how I planned to walk cross-country with less than a year's training. This time, I wasn't asking for their approval. I was accepting the position of Executive Director.

The Brides' March, once a fledgling idea met with raised eyebrows, now thrived, its scope far exceeding my initial vision. Rob Schroder's support, his unwavering belief when others dismissed me, had made this possible. Their initial reservations remained a vivid memory.

But each rejection had sharpened my focus, forcing me to refine my vision, to articulate it with greater clarity. The doubts of others had faded into the background, whispers against the roar of my own conviction.

Around the same time, in 2003, I received a call from a reporter with Marie Claire Magazine. I paused; my desk had several folders staring at me with applications to be filed on a homicide case that Mr. Butterworth wanted the Miami office to handle personally.

I fielded the reporter's questions, my voice tight with the effort of balancing the demands of career and home.

"What do you envision for the Brides' Walk?" she pressed. I could hear her pen scratching across what must have been very good quality paper. I closed my eyes, picturing it: a river of white, hundreds, perhaps thousands, of women in wedding gowns, their footsteps a unified rhythm against the devastating societal disease killing so many and transforming lives daily.

Less than ninety days later, I was on a flight to Washington, DC to meet with Mexican-American actress, director, and producer Salma Hayek. Marie Claire Magazine had ignited a spark; now, a procession bloomed.

Salma was a kind woman who was able to appreciate the vision, support the cause, and walk with us in a wedding gown screaming, "No more Violence Against Women."

I was moved by simply watching white cascade down the steps, a river of satin and lace flowing toward the heart of power, the heart of our country.

Wedding gowns, each a testament to a future without violence. I, who had once stood a solitary bride in the middle of Washington, DC, now found myself surrounded by a beautiful sea of men and women with a common goal: support the Ricart family in the midst of their grief and stand with us to say, "No more violence against women."

In the years since, men and women have joined our movement, sharing a common understanding, some using their celebrity status or political power to spread the word and elevate our work on a national and international platform. Our Brides' Walk, no matter the city or country, walk every step with a fierce resolve – a promise to walk the walk, not just speak it.

The New York City coalition, a bedrock of support that had cradled the Ricart family through the wreckage of tragedy and the sterile halls of justice, created this moment for us to be in the capital's shadow. The Ricart family, their presence a constant ache, present with us. For many, it was a reunion that tasted both sweet and sour.

The Ricart family has never shied away from showing us their grief and their emotional wounds. We walk, we talk, we weep, we hug, we wail, and even scream with sorrow, at times, but also with joy.

Their vulnerability has served as a model for the rest of the world to seek the strength that they need by exploring their pain and vulnerability in a safe environment amongst people who are emotionally healthier or at the very least, looking for healing.

Resilience is to continue living and moving forward after a tragedy. But healing is more than moving forward. The power of community healing provides an individual with the ability to restore, educate, and save others by using our truth and our testimonies, no matter how painful.

For the past 25 years, the Brides' March has continued its annual pilgrimage through Washington Heights, Upper Manhattan, Harlem, and The Bronx, its white tide a constant ebb and flow.

I work hard for every opportunity to attend as often as possible. I witnessed how the Washington Heights community, their collective heartbeats a steady rhythm, had grieved alongside the Ricart family. And in that shared space, beneath the ever-present chaos of the city, they continued to heal.

But as the movement grew, I began to crumble. In 2004, the panic attacks returned – the same ones that had plagued me as a child, the ones I thought professional success had cured. Severe depression. Anxiety that made it hard to breathe, hard to think, hard to be present with my daughters. I pushed through. I had to. There was no other option.

In 2007, I purchased a third home – proof, I thought, that I was thriving. The mortgage paperwork felt like another diploma.

See? I wanted to tell everyone. See how far I've come? A homeowner. A professional. A movement leader. The little Josie who was raped at nine had become someone who mattered.

And then came 2008.

The plasma donation center smelled like antiseptic and desperation. I lay on the vinyl bed, my arm extended, watching the needle slide into my vein. The machine hummed. My blood flowed out, clear and red, into the collection bag.

Forty-five minutes for forty dollars. Twice a week if my veins and iron levels could handle it.

Across from me, a young man with track marks scrolled through his phone. To my left, an elderly woman closed her eyes and seemed to be praying.

We didn't make eye contact. We were all here for the same reason: we needed the money more than we needed the plasma.

I thought about the college degrees, the awards, the movement I helped create. And here I was, selling my blood plasma to buy groceries because the 2008 global financial collapse had swallowed our third home, our car, our savings.

The machine beeped. The technician came over, removed the needle, pressed gauze against the puncture wound. "Keep pressure on it," she said, not unkindly.

I took my forty dollars in cash and drove to the gas station. I had a speaking engagement that evening at a domestic violence conference. I would stand on a stage in a hotel ballroom and talk about resilience, empowerment, healing. I would wear my good suit. No one would know that three hours earlier, I'd been lying on a vinyl bed selling my plasma.

Adrian and I barely spoke about the shame of it. We just kept moving, kept surviving, kept pretending everything was fine. We rode public transportation together. Visited food banks. Applied for assistance programs. And told no one. The facade of success at work remained intact. I was performing, always performing.

In 2010, our pastor intervened with a personal check for $5,000 to save the family home from foreclosure. We paid him back over the next year, but the depression only worsened. The panic attacks intensified. I began psychiatric treatment – medication, therapy, the whole clinical arsenal. Nothing helped.

One night, Adrian and I sat at the kitchen table after the girls had gone to bed. The house was quiet except for the hum of the refrigerator. We'd been married for twelve years. We'd survived financial collapse, my walk across the country, the demands of raising two daughters, the relentless pressure of my work. We were good partners. Good parents. Good friends.

"We're not really married anymore, are we?" I said.

He looked at me for a long moment. "No," he said quietly. "We're not."

"But we're staying."

"Yes."

We both knew why. It was comfortable. Familiar. Safe. We were better as friends than as lovers – we'd known that early on. My sexual trauma had made it difficult for us to share a solid intimate relationship. I'd tried. I'd failed. I'd stayed anyway because divorce felt like failure, catastrophe, proof that I couldn't make anything work, not even a marriage to a good man who loved me.

We stayed together, focused on growing, on helping others, on learning more. But we abandoned our marriage. I did not always feel safe with him, or maybe my body never felt safe with him, or anyone else for that matter. My body, just like my spirit, never had a steady home.

In 2011, I co-founded The College Brides' Walk, a movement that would expand domestic violence education across South Florida campuses. It started with a chance encounter in 2010 when my friend Sharon D'Eusanio couldn't make a speaking engagement and called me last-minute. "Can you do me a favor?" her voice crackled. "I'm so sorry, but I can't make it to this event. You'd be perfect."

That day, I met Dr. Mari Casares-Thorndike, Freddy Frage, and Dr. Laura Finley. After the final applause faded, mingling with the scent of stale coffee and nervous energy, a conversation ignited.

The four of us – a quartet drawn together by shared passion – began to weave the threads that would ultimately birth the College Brides' Walk during Teen Dating Violence Awareness Month.

It felt like the universe was saying: Keep going. Keep building. Keep creating healing spaces. So I did. Because that's what I knew how to do. I knew how to work. I knew how to serve. I knew how to put on the wedding gown and walk.

In 2012, I began my Master's in Clinical Mental Health Counseling. I was working full-time at the Department of Juvenile Justice. Raising two daughters. Running an international movement. Speaking at conferences, colleges, galas. Trying to save a marriage that had already ended. Trying to save myself without admitting I needed saving.

I didn't know it yet, but I was walking toward the edge of a cliff.

From the outside, it looked like success. Executive Director turned state employee turned graduate student. Movement leader. Activist invited to speak at prestigious events. The woman in the wedding gown who had walked 1,300 miles was now building an empire of awareness, education, advocacy.

But inside, I was still the nine-year-old girl who had never been allowed to weep after her rape. I was still the teenager who learned that survival meant numbing, performing, pretending. I was still the young woman who confused attention with love, accomplishment with healing, movement with progress.

The movement was growing. Brides' Marches multiplied across cities, states, countries. Thousands of women in wedding gowns walking in solidarity, raising awareness, creating healing tribes. The vision I'd received in Destin, Florida had become reality.

But I was dying inside. My body knew it even if my mind refused to admit it. The panic attacks were warnings. The depression was a siren. The inability to feel safe in my own marriage was a flashing red light.

I kept ignoring all of it. I kept walking, kept working, kept performing.

And in the spring of 2013, my body would finally force me to stop.

FIFTEEN
Spring 2013

Spring 2013. Fort Lauderdale.

I was working at the Florida Department of Juvenile Justice, as a Technical Assistance Specialist. I had recently resigned to a position with the Florida Attorney General's office in the Economic Crime Unit, where I was helping to disburse funding recovered for Florida citizens from the nationwide class action lawsuit against predatory lenders. I was working long hours. Attending Graduate school at night. Trying to be a mom, a wife, a granddaughter, a friend, a church member, a good neighbor.

I'm not exaggerating when I tell you I was trying to be and do all those things because all those roles were important to me.

I had a daughter in college and another daughter in high school. Adrian and I were still living together, still raising our girls together, still presenting as a family. But we weren't a couple. Not really. Not anymore.

One Wednesday night in March, I came home late from graduate school. Adrian was in the living room watching TV. The girls were in their rooms doing homework. I walked past him to the kitchen, heated up leftovers, ate standing at the counter. He didn't ask about my day. I didn't ask about his.

I washed my plate, put it in the dish rack, walked upstairs. We'd shared the same house for hours and spoken maybe ten words. 'Hi.' 'I'm going to bed?' 'Ok Mama', as he usually calls me. That was it. That was our marriage.

I lay in bed that night, Adrian asleep beside me, and felt more alone than I'd ever felt as a child. At least then, I knew I was alone. This was different. This was being alone while someone slept six inches away.

My marriage to Adrian, my rock, my best friend of fifteen years, crumbled like dry leaves underfoot. Our arguments turned into days of indifference. Polite greetings and obligatory goodbyes. We were not strangers; we became unknown to each other, unfamiliar, threatened by the thought of familiarity and the expectation behind the duty to resolve disagreements to clarify our relationship.

Adrian found it unnecessary. I found it indispensable. I was asking for something that he believed to be obvious by his deeds, but to me, I felt utterly alone in my mind, my body. I was suffocating.

We were great friends, awesome business partners, amazing co-parents, but the intimacy between us was complex, hard to describe, impossible to decipher. My trauma showed up in every room in my house. I say my trauma because that is the only trauma I know, and I know it well. Adrian did his best to help me, but this time, my trauma needed me, not him.

I decided to look for help. I scheduled a Saturday morning session with a psychologist recommended by my insurance. Fifteen years married, a beautiful home, two beautiful daughters, good job, great legacy with the Brides' Walk and everything happening in New York. Every year the movement was growing, but every year I was dying a little.

Gladys's death opened the door for me to examine my trauma. It triggered deep emotions, but I did nothing. Nothing showed me how much I needed to work through. The worst thing you can do is nothing. At least when it comes to mental health and trauma. Nothing is contraindicated. Nothing can kill you or others. Nothing is dangerous.

Her office was in a professional building off Federal Highway. Beige walls, leather furniture, a box of tissues strategically placed on the coffee table. She was a middle-aged woman with glasses and a notepad. I sat on the couch. She sat in the chair across from me.

"Tell me what brings you in today," she said.

I talked for maybe fifteen minutes. The marriage. The silence. The loneliness. The sense that I was failing at everything despite accomplishing so much. The exhaustion. The panic attacks that had returned. The depression that sat on my chest every morning when I woke up.

She took notes. Nodded occasionally. Asked a few clarifying questions. And then she put down her pen and looked at me with what I can only describe as clinical detachment.

"Your marriage is over," she said. "What are you waiting for to leave?"

I stared at her. "I... what?"

"You just described a dead marriage. You're not getting what you need. He's not interested in changing. So why are you still there?"

"Because I have two daughters," I said, my voice shaking. "Because I made a commitment. Because I don't know how to—"

"Those are excuses," she interrupted. "You're using your daughters as an excuse to avoid doing the hard thing. That's not fair to them or to you."

The room tilted. I'd come looking for a witness, someone to bear witness to the tremors in my voice, the unshed tears welling in my eyes. I'd come looking for help navigating the pain. Instead, she was telling me the marriage was dead and I was a coward for not leaving.

"I think we should explore why you feel abandoned," I tried to explain my feelings, my outlook. I remember saying, "I think maybe if I understood my own patterns—"

"Brutal honesty," she said, leaning forward. "That's what I offer. Your truth. And your truth is that you're clinging to something that's already gone."

I stood up. My legs felt unsteady. "Thank you for your time," I said.

"Think about what I said," she called after me as I walked out.

I made it to my car before the panic hit. Full-body shaking. Gasping for air. The parking lot spinning. My hands gripping the steering wheel so hard my knuckles turned white.

"Your marriage is over. What are you waiting for to leave?"

The words looped in my head. Over and over. Over and over. I'd come seeking help and been told the one stable thing in my life – my marriage to Adrian, my partnership, my co-parent, my friend – was dead. And it was my fault for not having the courage to bury it.

I started the car and drove home. I entered the house and sat in my room for hours. Breathing became difficult and I could not stop crying. Adrian sat with me for some time, he tried to comfort me, but I couldn't be consoled. I stood up and ended up driving to Broward General Medical Center instead.

I didn't want to die. Not this time. But I also didn't know how to continue living with the profound feeling of failure and abandonment that was crushing my chest. I walked into the emergency room and told the receptionist, "I need help. I'm not safe."

They admitted me to the crisis unit. Three days. A small room with a bed, a chair, a window with bars. The overwhelming weight of her blunt assessment, the deep emotional emptiness, sent me spiraling.

It was a replay of my teenage years, the same desolate feeling of hopelessness, the same exhaustion – this time, Jackson Memorial Hospital's crisis unit a faded photograph in the album of my pain.

The first day was intake. Assessments. Questions. Medication. A nurse who spoke softly and didn't rush me when I cried. A social worker who asked about my support system. I told her I had Adrian and the girls. She asked if Adrian knew I was here. I said no, not yet.

The second day, I met Dr. Sobhan. He was a man in his fifties with kind eyes and an unhurried way of speaking. He pulled up a chair beside my bed rather than sitting behind a desk. That small gesture – choosing to sit with me rather than across from me – made me cry.

"Tell me what happened," he said.

I told him about the therapist. About her words. About the panic in the parking lot. About how I'd driven here instead of home because I didn't trust myself to be alone.

He listened without interrupting. When I finished, he was quiet for a moment. Then he said, "You did exactly the right thing by coming here. You recognized you needed help and you asked for it. That takes tremendous courage."

"I don't feel courageous," I said. "I feel like a failure."

"You are not a failure," he said, and the way he said it – calm, certain, like he was stating a fact rather than offering an opinion – made me believe him, at least for a moment. "You are enough. You have always been enough. And you will get through this."

Over the next two days, Dr. Sobhan became the anchor in my turbulent recovery. He didn't preach or patronize. He didn't offer easy answers. Instead, his gaze, calm and unwavering, acknowledged the battlefield of my soul.

He handed me the medication information sheet, which was a nod to my agency, my right to understand and choose. He helped me see that the therapist's brutal honesty wasn't honesty at all – it was judgment masquerading as clinical assessment.

"Your marriage may be struggling," he said. "But that doesn't make you a coward. And it doesn't mean the only answer is to leave. You get to decide what healing looks like for you."

The hope he helped me unearth wasn't some fairy tale, but a fragile seedling I carefully nurtured, a tiny green shoot pushing through the cracked earth of my trauma.

Spring became summer. Summer became fall. I continued taking the medication Dr. Sobhan prescribed. Continued going to graduate school. Continued working at the Department of Juvenile Justice. Continued helping grow the Brides' March movement. Continued living with Adrian and raising our daughters.

I was experiencing depression and anxiety, but at least now I was under care. Dr. Sobhan and I met monthly. The medication helped take the edge off the panic. But the exhaustion remained. The sense of fraudulence remained. The feeling that I was one misstep away from collapse remained.

All of my insecurities were thriving during this time. "Who do you think you are going to grad school? You will fail just like you failed law school!" I tried to go to law school in 2008 and was suspended for a year after being 2 points short on my GPA. I never went back, feeling defeated and dealing with our financial crisis instead. Now that voice was back, louder than ever.

Work became my coping mechanism again. If I was busy enough, productive enough, accomplished enough, maybe I wouldn't have to feel the emptiness.

My body had other plans.

October 13th, 2013.

I'd been scheduled for a business trip to Tallahassee, about six hours away from home. Three days of meetings with our new supervisor, delivering a presentation in front of my colleagues for evaluation and feedback.

My leg had been hurting for a while – a dull, persistent ache on my calf that made me limp. I dismissed it as a consequence of ill-fitting heels and the extra weight I'd gained since starting the psychotropic medication.

My breath had been shallow for days. I told myself it was stress. The new supervisor. The presentation I had to give.

But the truth, hidden beneath the flimsy layers of self-deception, was far more sinister. My body was fighting a silent war, and I was too busy to listen.

The drive from Tallahassee to Fort Lauderdale blurred into a landscape of pain. Every breath hurt. My leg throbbed. I had to stop twice to rest because I was so lightheaded. But I made it to the government building to return the State car.

I unloaded the equipment and headed towards my office from the parking lot. Adrian was picking up Savannah from a dance recital. I was going to wait for them both to pick me up from work.

I walked slowly through the parking lot to catch my breath. The earth started spinning. My chest felt like someone was standing on it. I couldn't get air. Not like a panic attack – I knew what those felt like. This was different. This was my body shutting down. I collapsed and lost consciousness. When I woke up, my pants were soiled and my glasses were knocked off my face.

I called 911.

The operator's voice, a calm island in the storm of my chest, stayed with me as I gasped for breath. Each second felt like an eternity until the distant wail of sirens, growing closer, then faltering. The ambulance was unable to access the parking lot. I could hear them on the phone with the operator, trying to find the gate.

I called Adrian. "I'm at work. I called 911. The ambulance can't enter the building. Can you–" My breath gave out.

"I'm coming," he said. "Hold on. I'm coming."

Adrian's arrival was a relief. I saw him outside the parking lot entering the code to open the gate and let the ambulance in the building. Before the heavy doors of the fire truck even creaked open, I saw him – a paramedic, a blur of motion, vaulting over the fence like a superhero from a half-remembered childhood cartoon.

He knelt beside me, his questions a jumble of words I struggled to comprehend, my answers fragmented, gasps for air interspersed with broken, incoherent sentences. Adrian, now beside me, became the bridge between my struggling breaths and the medical team.

"She has anxiety," Adrian said, the words sharp and clear against the background hum of emergency lights.

I met the paramedic's gaze, defiance flickering in my eyes. "Never peed my pants. Never fainted." But then I remembered, I had fainted but never peed my pants. The more I tried to talk the less I could breathe. He told me to stop talking and focus on slowing down my breath. His eyes, focused and professional, quickly flicked to the oxygen monitor, then the blood pressure cuff. His expression changed. "We need to go. Now."

The world blurred. A whirlwind of efficient, precise actions: the straps of the stretcher, the oxygen mask, the IV line. The siren. The lights. Adrian's hand holding mine in the ambulance.

Hours later, the diagnosis, a stark, brutal sentence: severe pulmonary embolism. A heart infarct. A deadly journey of a blood clot from a deep vein in my leg, traveling through my bloodstream, blocking the lifeblood to my heart and lungs. The doctor's face was grim. "You're very lucky," he said. "This could have killed you."

They kept me in the hospital for about three days. Blood thinners. Monitoring. Tests. The girls came to visit, their faces pale with fear. Stephanie stayed the night with me. Savannah held my hand; she had to endure watching her father help the ambulance find me and then carry me on the stretcher. Adrian sat in the chair beside me.

"You have to slow down," he said on the third day. "You can't keep doing this to yourself."

"I know," I said.

But I didn't know. Not really. Because four months later, in February 2014, I would have a second pulmonary embolism. That's when they diagnosed me with Protein S Deficiency, a genetic blood clotting disorder. That's when they told me I would be on blood thinners for the rest of my life.

My body, ignored and neglected, had finally roared its protest. The fear of bad news, the constant pain, the nagging worry... I'd been too busy to listen. Work, cleaning, kids, driving, cooking, celebrating, studying, presenting, marching, advocating – a whirlwind of responsibilities, a carefully constructed wall against the quiet voice of my own exhaustion.

I couldn't afford to be sick. So, my life decided to handle me.

The pattern was becoming clearer, even if I couldn't fully see it yet:

Spring 2013: Mental health breakdown. Three days in psychiatric ward. Dr. Sobhan offers anchor, prescribes medication, teaches me I'm enough.

Fall 2013: Pulmonary embolism. Heart infarct. Nearly died because I ignored my body's warnings.

February 2014: Second pulmonary embolism. Protein S Deficiency diagnosis. Blood thinners for life.

May 2014: Graduated with my Master's in Clinical Mental Health Counseling. Another accomplishment. Another degree.

The pattern: I would work myself to collapse. My body would force me to stop. I would recover just enough to start the cycle again. Accomplish, collapse, recover, repeat.

Adrian and I continued living together, raising our daughters, maintaining the facade. The marriage was over. We both knew it. We just didn't know how to end it without destroying the fragile stability we'd built for Stephanie and Savannah.

So we didn't end it. We just kept pretending. Kept functioning and surviving.

I wasn't fine. My body had tried to kill me twice in six months. My marriage was a shell. My mental health required daily medication and monthly therapy just to keep me upright.

But I was very good at pretending.

And I would keep pretending for one more year, until my body gave me a gift I never asked for and didn't know how to receive: my third daughter, Sophia.

SIXTEEN
Sophia

Spring 2014. I sat in Dr. Tache's office, the hematologist who had diagnosed me with Protein S Deficiency after my second pulmonary embolism in February.

"Do you plan on having more children?" he asked.

I explained that Adrian and I had been trying for ten years without success. At forty-two, with two pulmonary embolisms behind me, a genetic blood clotting disorder, and a marriage that had emotionally ended years ago, pregnancy wasn't something I contemplated anymore.

"Good," Dr. Tache said. "Because due to the blood clotting condition caused by Protein S Deficiency and your age, pregnancy is not advisable." He was firm. I didn't ask for details, nor did I need to.

The conversation ended there.

Spring 2015. I was forty-three years old.

Roger and I had been friends for almost a decade. It was never romantic. But in the spring of 2015, we started spending time together. What happened wasn't planned. What happened was two people searching for connection in all the wrong ways, for all the wrong reasons.

In May, I found out I was pregnant.

I sat in my car in the pharmacy parking lot, staring at the positive test, thinking about Dr. Tache's warning: "Pregnancy is not advisable." I thought about Adrian, how we raised Savannah together, still presented as a family. I thought about Stephanie, twenty-three, and Savannah, eighteen, and what this would mean for them.

I called Roger. He said he would support me in whatever choice I made. Having a child with me wasn't his intention. It wasn't mine either.

Roger came with me to see Dr. Tache. The moment I walked into the office, I could see Dr. Tache was not happy.

"I thought we discussed how pregnancy was not advisable," he said.

He asked me directly: Did I want to keep the baby?

I explained that I had never ended a pregnancy before and even the thought of it made me very uncomfortable. The word itself felt foreign, impossible. Having Sophia was never a question for me. Terminating the pregnancy and hiding it from everyone would probably make my life easier, but I have never taken the easy way out. Every struggle I've faced head-on has helped me develop character and integrity.

I contemplated the thought of not having her for about an hour, but I couldn't conceive of it. Terminating the pregnancy would be terminating me, my destiny, because the moment she was conceived she became a part of me and a part of my future. That, I knew firmly. And to me, that is all that mattered.

Dr. Tache explained that pregnancy in my condition would be high risk. I would need to inject blood thinners two or three times per day to avoid blood clots but not bleed to death if I had a miscarriage or went into labor. It was a delicate balance that nobody had insight about except for my doctor, his assistant, and myself.

"This is dangerous," he said. "You understand that?"

"I understand," I said.

But I wasn't scared of having her. If I bled to death, the thought was not scary to me. I was not defiant. I was not out to prove anything to anyone. I did not have her to gain power. I had her to have inner peace, no matter the cost.

I knew it was going to be hard. I knew I was going to be judged. I knew I was going to lose respect, friendships, and even influence in the field of activism, school, and work. But truly, my main concern was continuing to lose myself.

My marriage had ended. I figured if I was pregnant as a result of consciously engaging in a sexual relationship with someone I care about and respect, then I helped forge my own destiny. I was not afraid of the consequences, but I was keenly aware of the cost I was getting ready to pay.

After praying about my decision, there was not a moment I contemplated not having her. But there were many moments when I counted the cost – financially, spiritually, and emotionally. Every time, the answer was the same: "I can't afford not to have her, even if it kills me."

Soon after telling Roger and visiting Dr. Tache, I talked to Adrian. I explained that I was pregnant.

His response: "I will support you."

I explained it was Roger's baby and staying in the house was not going to help me emotionally. I found a small efficiency and moved out.

I talked to my daughters. Stephanie, twenty-three. Savannah, eighteen. Two young women, confused and disappointed, carrying some of my shame even though they wouldn't admit it. I knew they did.

During my pregnancy, I must have injected myself over four hundred times. Daily injections of blood thinners to keep my blood thin enough to avoid blood clots but not too thin to hemorrhage. My belly was often severely bruised due to my clumsiness injecting myself.

I continued to work full-time at the Department of Juvenile Justice. I was enrolled at FIU during the entire pregnancy in order to graduate with my Master's degree. It was not easy. I was not trying to be a hero. I just kept moving aimlessly to do what needed to be done. I was feeling the pain, the struggle, the uncertainty, but I had to keep moving. To me, stopping meant death. Contemplating was going to bring me back to a feeling of shame and despair that was too hard for me to even conceive.

I was abandoned and chastised by friends, family members, and church members. I never told anyone that this was Adrian's child. As my belly grew, I would run into church members or neighbors or coworkers who would ask, and I always made it crystal clear that it was not Adrian's child – which automatically made me a cheater, an adulterous woman.

Neighbors, church members, co-workers, and many others saw me as what I had become, or at least what I showed the world that I was: an adulterous woman without self-respect.

Nobody in my family offered to have a baby shower. My work wanted to give me one and I refused. I didn't have many friends, and those that I did have judged me harshly to my face, which led to four severe panic attacks – three at a restaurant and the other, stemming from losing my closest friend, recurrent for over a year.

My divorce to Adrian was finalized before Sophia was born.

"I'll always be your friend," he said. "I'll always be Savannah's father. And I'll always care about you. But we can't keep pretending we're married when we're not."

"I know," I said.

"And Josie? This baby deserves a mother who's fully present. Not one who's exhausted from pretending."

He was right. He was always right about things like that.

December 30, 2015, a month before the due date, I went into labor.

The medical team was ready. Dr. Tache had prepared a protocol. The obstetrician knew the risks. I was monitored constantly, blood thinners adjusted, every vital sign tracked. The delivery had to be carefully managed – too much bleeding could kill me, but stopping the blood thinners too soon could cause a fatal clot.

Roger was out of town. I contacted him briefly to inform him that Sophia had her own timetable. Adrian stepped in like the hero he has always been in my life. We were both terrified, we knew the risk, and this was too soon.

Adrian was with me throughout the entire pregnancy, watching my belly grow, touching her through my skin, talking to Sophia and falling in love with her, one soft kick at a time. Adrian held us from beginning to end, he loved Sophia before she was born, as much as I did. We held hands, terrified, but present.

After 10 agonizing hours in labor, the doctor called for an emergency c-section. I had never experienced surgery in my life and this was not a moment I was looking forward to. Dr. Tache told me, whatever you do, make sure you don't have a C-section. Well, that obviously was not up to me and we both knew it.

Stephanie and Savannah were in the birthing suite, my dear friend Sonia arrived shortly after Pastor Johnson. We began praying and worshipping God; the same God Mama introduced me to when

I was a child. The same God that sustained me through abuse. The same God that gave life to Sophia and multiply my faith to have her.

As the medical team announced they were ready, Adrian entered the operating room with me, not leaving my side.

A few minutes later, in my mind anyway, our beautiful Sophia was born.

Perfect. Healthy. Alive.

I was conscious, completely aware, I heard her cries and watched Adrian cut her umbilical cord. He held her in his arms and watched her with love in his eyes. I was overwhelmed by his love. A love that was photographed by the nurses, a love that came through even in photos.

He placed her in my arms, and I held her against my chest, this tiny miracle, this unexpected gift, this baby I'd risked my life to bring into the world. I had injected myself over four hundred times. I endured shame, judgment, rejection. I had lost friendships, respect, and influence. I had watched my daughters' eyes filled with confusion and at times disappointment.

And it was worth it. Because she was here. And she was a gift that I couldn't refuse. Roger arrived shortly after her birth and stayed the night, loving on her and helping me feed her. I was completely exhausted, but I wanted to make sure her first feedings were breast milk and not formula.

Adrian came to the hospital the next day, holding flowers, looking at Sophia with the same gentle expression he'd had when Savannah was born eighteen years earlier.

"She's beautiful," he said. "Congratulations, Josie."

"Will you be her Godfather?" I asked.

He smiled. "Of course."

I had moved back into the family home before Sophia was born. Adrian and Savannah didn't want me to be alone during the pregnancy and with a newborn, especially given my health. So we figured it out. Divorced, but living in the same house. Co-parenting Savannah. Both of us helping with Sophia. It was unconventional. It was complicated. It was messy. But it worked.

Roger and I co-parented Sophia together. He loved her. He showed up. He was present. Adrian became her Godfather and treated her with genuine care.

I am the mother of three daughters with three different fathers. Society has words for women like me. The church has words for women like me. I faced shame daily from people who didn't understand my behaviors, my failures, my disgrace. Or what they saw as disgrace.

As a trauma survivor, I could have used drugs. I could have turned to crime. I could have succumbed to my mental health struggles. I could have been 750 pounds from eating my emotions. I could have been serving a life sentence for killing Mike.

Instead, I had three daughters. Stephanie, a college graduate working in the arts. Savannah, beginning her own journey as a vocalist. And Sophia, who would one day give me the tremendous honor of loving her like a healthy mother should.

But I wasn't healed yet. Not even close.

The shame would deepen. The depression would crush me. The self-criticism would become unbearable. I would numb the pain through overwork, through alcohol, through nicotine, through anything that would let me stop feeling.

I had Sophia. But she did not have me yet. I had not learned how to be the mother she deserved. People were not kinder to me once she was born. I was not kinder to myself either.

That lesson would take seven more years of suffering.

Seven years of proving to myself, over and over, that I was exactly what everyone said I was: not enough. Not worthy. Not deserving of love or peace or rest.

Until one winter night in 2022, when Sophia would stand in front of me, look me in the eyes, and ask me to come inside, and I would finally hear her.

SEVENTEEN
Palm Beach

The years between 2016 and 2019 blur together now. Work, bed, work. A bottle of wine. A pack of cigarettes. Back to bed until it was time to go to work again. I hated myself and most things around me.

My foundation – emotional, physical, even spiritual – was severely fractured. The exhaustion wasn't just tiredness; it was a bone-deep weariness, a constant low hum of emotional pain and disappointment that vibrated in my muscles until it reached my bones. I felt every one of my years etched into my face – a roadmap of disappointments.

Two broken marriages. Three daughters, three different fathers – each a tear in the fabric of my life. The ghost of abandoned childhood clung to me, a chill even the Florida sun couldn't dispel. Shame, a familiar shadow, stretched long and dark.

I didn't understand it then, but the internal screams of my body were the signs of unprocessed childhood trauma coming to the surface, just like the Adverse Childhood Study predicted.

During my early thirties, I had been diagnosed with Vitiligo, an autoimmune disorder causing my body to see the pigmentation on my skin as a threat. The disorder leaves the body disfigured with discolored skin.

The more stress I encountered, the faster the disorder moved through my body. My skin was becoming a map of my internal chaos, a visible testament to the war being waged within. Another way for my body to tell my story.

Numbing became my survival strategy. Alcohol dulled the shame. Nicotine punctuated the hours. Overwork provided the perfect excuse to avoid feeling anything at all. I showed up for others – always showing up for others – while my own inner turmoil raged unchecked.

The numbing helped me survive, but it prevented me from living.

Stephanie and Savannah were grown women by then, capable of forming their own judgments. And they had. I felt them pulling away, their respect for me crumbling with each passing month. I had lost not just their honesty – they guarded their truths from me now – but something even more precious: their belief in who I had been to them.

They needed guidance – women in their twenties navigating their own relationships, their own questions about love and commitment – but I didn't feel worthy of offering it. How could I? I was the cautionary tale, not the mentor. What wisdom could I possibly share? Don't do what I did wasn't exactly the legacy I had hoped to leave them.

Savannah was graduating High School that Summer and I was helping her get ready for prom. I remember inviting one of her mentors to help us. As I walked across the living room, I watched my reflection in the mirror. How was I going to help my young daughter transition into a young adult while my own behavior was immature and reckless?

I missed the mark, often. And once I realized my mistakes, I would be useless for weeks. The internal critic was relentless: Who do you think you are? You will fail just like you failed law school. You failed your marriages. You failed your daughters.

This constant internal conflict was breaking me. All of my insecurities were thriving during this time.

In 2020, when the world shut down, I took a sabbatical.

COVID gave everyone permission to pause, and I seized it. I stayed in the family home — that strange unconventional environment I shared with Adrian — and tried to begin healing. Tried to redefine my goals. Tried to remember who I was before the shame had become my second skin. It was the first time in years I had stopped long enough to hear my own thoughts, and what I heard terrified me.

The sabbatical helped, but it wasn't enough. I was still living in the architecture of my old life, surrounded by the reminders of everything I had lost and everything I had done wrong.

Adrian and I had managed to transform our relationship into something even more complex. I grew more despondent, felt more abrasive, less feminine, apart from myself more and more. I found myself feeling abandoned, not by Adrian, but the self, by God. I also started feeling like a burden. The healing I needed required a change of geography.

In 2021, I moved to West Palm Beach with Sophia.

She was five years old – this unexpected grace, this symbol of both my greatest shame and my deepest blessing. We left the family home, left the proximity to Adrian and the girls, left the geography of my indiscretions. I told myself it was a fresh start. I told myself I was starting over.

What I didn't realize was that you can't outrun your own shadow. The past, the shame, the narrative, it all traveled with me. The depression came along for the ride. But there was one thing waiting for me in Palm Beach that would change everything – though I didn't know it yet.

Her name was Carol Brown.

I met her at the Palm Beach Courthouse, where I had taken a position as a Victim's Advocate after my ten months sabbatical. Mrs. Brown, as we called her in the hallowed halls of our shared professional life, radiated an unshakeable serenity. Her wisdom was a breath of fresh air for some of us and unnerving chaos for others. She had a way of asking exactly the question you were afraid to answer.

She became my supervisor. She became my mentor. She became, in many ways, the spiritual guide I didn't know I needed, badly – a new chapter of spiritual growth beginning to unfold even as everything else felt like it was falling apart.

My initial role as Victim's Advocate was a welcome haven, a chance to rebuild, by revisiting my professional roots.

Every day, the morning sun greeted me through my wall-to-wall office window, touching everything on my desk and becoming part of my grounding routine. "Remember to feel the sun on your skin," I would tell myself daily. This office – decorated with personal artifacts, co-workers' gifts, and professional mementos – was not just my workplace. It was part of my identity. An extension of everything I had worked and studied for.

The scent of peppermint from the diffuser mingled with the faint aroma of old books, a deliberate attempt to create a space where even the most shattered spirits could find a moment's peace.

My caseload was a complex tapestry of suffering: stalking, sexual assault, domestic violence, the insidious creep of elder exploitation, and homicide cases. Faces flashed before my eyes – a young mother clutching a child, a stooped elderly man, the hollow-eyed gaze of a young man who spoke only Spanish. Each day I received calls – a whispered Spanish plea for help, the choked sobs of a young woman.

In the occasional, hesitant smile of a survivor, I found something deeper than just relief: a profound and humbling sense of purpose. The intersection of hope and despair? I knew it intimately. It was the very street I walked down every day. Not for me, but for others. This is why it felt so familiar, so comfortable, so safe.

When the sole Spanish-speaking therapist resigned – a cascade of whispered anxieties in the breakroom, the hurried shuffle of papers as her case files were reassigned – it left a gaping hole. Administration's request felt like a great opportunity.

"Can you help with the Spanish-speaking clients?" I nodded eagerly. "Of course! Thank you for asking. I'd be happy to help." It felt like a chance to start practicing mental health again and positioning myself as a team player.

As I started working both jobs – victim advocate during the day and therapist at night – my life evolved into my old routine. No time for me, for my girls, for my life. But this was a new job. I needed to prove myself. I needed to show them how good I was.

Evenings blurred into a haze of Spanish and English, therapy notes and advocacy reports. Self-care, once a carefully planned ritual, became a fleeting memory as I navigated the emotional minefield of both roles. A faint sense of purpose transformed into exhaustion.

I was falling back into my oldest pattern: serving others to avoid feeling anything at all. The numbness was comfort, a familiar blanket against the void. The more I did, the less I existed.

It had been almost ten years since the marriage ended. Ten years of grieving what we had built, what we had lost, what I had destroyed.

Adrian and I maintained our strange choreography – Sophia's father Roger co-parenting with us, Adrian still serving as her Godfather, the boundaries between past and present constantly blurring. We had been best friends for fifteen years. Now we were... something else. Something without a name. My daughters continued their slow thaw, but trust, once broken, repairs itself in inches, not miles.

I tried to launch my mental health practice. I tried to regain my confidence, my self-respect. But my health continued to deteriorate. The stress fed the autoimmune disorder, which fed the shame, which fed the depression, which fed the stress. A vicious cycle with no clear exit.

Yet there were islands of pride in that turbulent sea.

The awards still shimmered on my desk – cold metal trophies reflecting years of tireless work. The painting from the National Organization for Women Intrepid Awards. The delicate crystal from the Florida International Torch Awards. The beautiful piece from the Broward County Crisis Unit Employee of the Year Award.

I had helped build systems, crafted programs, shaped policies – lifelines for juveniles and adults snared in the legal net.

The international movement against domestic violence, that was my legacy. A legacy I helped establish. A legacy I had walked thousands of miles in my wedding gown to ignite. I had done that. I changed the conversation about domestic violence and created a community healing movement. I had given countless survivors hope.

And yet.

I felt like a complete failure. I felt like all that professional success meant nothing when I couldn't hold my own life together. When I couldn't look at myself in the mirror without flinching. The paradox was crushing: I had helped establish an international movement, but I couldn't save myself from my own darkness.

By the end of 2021, I was professionally tired, surrounded by success, awards, achievements – and yet feeling irrelevant.

The usual pride I felt – a pride built over nearly three decades, honed in the Miami-Dade and Broward State Attorney's Offices, the Attorney General's office, the Department of Juvenile Justice, and the victim services of Palm Beach and Broward Counties – felt distant. My professional ego was bruised, deeply.

Twenty-eight years spent navigating the wreckage of other people's lives – the raw wounds left by violence, the chilling aftermath etched onto faces and souls. I'd seen things that would curdle milk. But the devastation was starting to feel personal. An unfamiliar knot of professional anxiety, a suffocating imposter syndrome, tightened its grip.

The whispers started in September 2022, a few months after my 50th birthday.

Two young therapists, their eyes narrowed with a curiosity that felt like suspicion, kept circling back to my license. Their questions, precise, were never directed at me. They never warned me or encouraged me to look into it, to renew, to be mindful. Instead of asking if I was aware of my professional shortcomings, they spoke to administration.

The resentment had been simmering, invisible – at least to me – as a few co-workers saw me thrive within the office. Their glances, sharp and calculating, were the tiny daggers of workplace politics. I had been so focused on my caseload, on proving myself, on showing them how good I was, that I had completely missed the deadlines.

My role – advocate, witness, protector – felt both immense and acutely fragile. Later, the weight of death pressed down. A mother's heartbroken wail echoed in my ears as I delivered the news at 4:00 AM that her son was killed while riding his motorcycle by a drunk driver. The paperwork for the Victim Compensation Fund blurred – funeral expenses, relocation, counseling – a cascade of costs born from violence.

September arrived, and the new Mental Health supervisor asked to meet with me.

Her voice, crisp and official, sliced through the quiet.

"Your license. It expired in March. You were practicing without a license."

The words hit me like a bucket of ice. The room tilted. The air was hard to inhale. A dizzying wave crashed over me, washing away my carefully constructed professional composure.

"I... I renewed it," I stammered, my voice unconvincing even to myself.

The paperwork and the official stamps suddenly felt like they had no real value. The carefully cultivated calm I'd built around myself crumbled, revealing the fragile foundation beneath.

"Josie, your license has expired." The Florida Department of Health website, a cold digital judgment, flashed before my eyes.

"How do you know?" I managed to respond, the words tasting like defeat.

"The other two therapists searched the health department database and realized that your license was expired," she explained.

Every past failure, every whisper of self-doubt, rose up to crucify me.

Who do you think you are? The familiar question, a phantom voice, sliced through me. My meticulously constructed academic achievements, once a source of strength, now felt like fragile towers built on shifting sand.

I felt every day of those fifty years I had just celebrated – a roadmap of disappointments. The ghost of abandoned childhood clung to me.

I was accused of practicing without a license without a single consideration that I was overwhelmed trying to help Spanish-speaking clients and completely missed the deadlines.

These two therapists had no idea of my past trauma. They had no concept of what it took for me to believe in myself enough to go to graduate school, to pursue a career in helping others despite my own need for healing. I didn't have many of the privileges that they had, but they did not need to know all that.

My carefully constructed professional identity – the scaffolding of my life – began to crumble.

The kindness of some of my other co-workers, their concern only amplified the pain. They had seen my accomplishments, my dedication. Now, they saw my vulnerability. I felt burdened by their concern and my own failure.

I ran to my faith. Then I ran to my therapist.

Her virtual couch became my refuge. Each session was a slow, agonizing excavation, unearthing the fragile foundation of my self-worth. I realized, with a sickening lurch in my stomach, that my professional life had become my entire life. Without it, I was... nothing.

Carol, my supervisor, her hand firm and warm in mine, navigated me through the storm. "What do you want?" she asked, her voice a steady anchor in the turbulent sea of my anxieties.

Kate, my clinical supervisor, her unwavering gaze helped me confront discomfort, to stand firm in the face of the accusations. Her guidance gave me the strength to submit the paperwork, re-activate my license, and restore my professional credentials. She asked me to be reminded of who I am.

"I am, I will always be, an advocate for victims."

This truth, a stubborn ember, refused to be extinguished.

But months bled into each other, a relentless cycle of despair.

November 30th, 2022.

The office Christmas party loomed – a social obligation I dreaded more than any court appearance. Those two therapists were going to be there. The entire office could see me and judge me. I didn't want to attend, but I forced myself to go. To hide would be to admit defeat.

I survived the party. Barely.

December 1st, 2022. The date felt insignificant, except for all the heavy foot traffic radiating from the Palm Beach Courthouse during the holiday season.

I parked on the fifth-floor parking and walked through the overhead crossway to avoid the metallic shriek of train tracks directly across from the courthouse. The endless shuffle of the security line – a sea of faces blurred by time constraints and unmet deadlines.

"Good morning," I mumbled, the words automatically responding to the eye contact of complete strangers. Several visitors needed guidance through the security maze; I mechanically directed them.

This wasn't the usual morning. This was... different. A deep fatigue settled in my bones, a weight heavier than any case file. The usual pride I felt – a pride built over nearly three decades, honed in the government buildings across South Florida felt... distant. My professional ego, bruised, deeply.

The memory of my seventeen-year-old self, navigating jail lobbies and courtrooms to bail out my mother, flashed unexpectedly bright. The pleading in my voice as I addressed the judge, begging for treatment instead of release, still resonated.

But that was then. Now, December 1st, 2022, removed from other people's problems, as a full-grown adult, I should feel strong, independent, completely confident, right?

Gasping slightly, I reached my office.

I performed the body scan I routinely teach my clients – the familiar ritual of checking in with physical sensations. My breath was dysregulated. I could feel it. I was professionally tired, surrounded by success, awards, achievements – and yet feeling irrelevant.

I've witnessed anxiety in countless clients, the high-stakes tension of impending trials, depositions, restraining orders – I understood the tremors, the clammy hands, the hollow eyes. But this... this was alien, both to my experience and my expertise.

The grounding exercises were not working.

My hands, slick with a cold sweat, fumbled at the keyboard. Each keystroke felt like a lead weight. I felt my chest squeeze, as if my rib cage were closing in and squeezing my lungs.

What the hell Josie? Again? come on breathe, relax! I am safe, I am at work, come on!!!

I walked to Carol's office, a space of sanity and calm amidst the bureaucratic storm.

Mrs. Brown, as we called her in the hallowed halls of our shared professional life, radiated an unshakeable serenity. Her wisdom was a breath of fresh air for some of us and unnerving chaos for others. I entered her office and sat without asking for permission.

Without turning away from her computer screen, she asked, "Did you enjoy the Christmas party last night?" She chuckled, her voice warm, unaware of the distraught look on my face.

We shared a few easy moments of deep breathing as she turned to see me. A few seconds from the tempest within. The tension, a vise around my heart, began to loosen, ever so slightly.

Back at my desk, the email sat waiting.

Several months of research, phone calls, and completed forms culminated in this one digital communication. My fingers trembled as I clicked it open. The words swam before my eyes, blurring the edges of my vision.

"Congratulations..."

The rest dissolved into a wash of relief.

A tremor ran through me. My knees buckled, giving way under the bulk of years of effort, years of doubt, finally, gloriously, validated. Tears, hot and unrestrained, streamed down my face. Twenty-eight years distilled to this one sentence, a life's work reaffirmed in a simple, understated email from the Florida Department of Health.

Within the privacy of my office and the familiar indifferent silence standing next to me, only the soft, ragged sound of my own weeping remained.

The exemption clause, a small paragraph buried deep within the legal jargon, explained everything. A counselor does not need a license to practice for a nonprofit and a government agency in Florida.

I wasn't practicing illegally.

The relief was a physical collapse. On my knees, tears streamed down my face, a prayer escaping my lips.

I forwarded the email to Carol.

Her footsteps, quick and urgent, echoed down the hallway. In my office, her congratulatory words were lost in the strangled gasp that tore from my throat.

Pain lanced through my neck, radiating outwards. Panic, raw and terrifying, enveloped me. Two pulmonary embolisms haunted my past; I couldn't risk another self-diagnosis.

"Carol..." I choked out, each word a struggle.

Her face paled.

"Ambulance!" she yelled, her voice sharp and clear, cutting through the fog of my terror.

The gurney felt cold and unforgiving beneath me.

The courthouse, once a place of strength and purpose, became a stage for my humiliation. The stares of my colleagues, faces blurred through a veil of tears and pain, etched themselves into my memory.

Personal vulnerability was familiar. But this... this professional vulnerability was a horrifying new landscape. It was terrifying. It was scary.

This is the day everything started to change.

Severe panic attack confirmed my fragile professional identity and my lack of integration and wholeness. My life was compartmentalized based on roles, parts, identities – not wholeness. I was the advocate. The therapist. The activist. The mother. The survivor. The ex-wife. The ex-lover. I was everything to everyone but I was not me, not even to me. I had never learned to be just me.

The paradox that had been crushing me for years finally cracked open: I had helped others begin their healing journey, but I had never done the work to heal myself.

For over twenty years, I had chosen work and achievement and service to others over the terrifying prospect of facing my own wounds.

Now, lying in a hospital bed after a panic attack that my colleagues had witnessed, I couldn't continue to ignore my needs anymore.

Something had to change.

But before the change could come, I would have to experience something deep within to generate the inspiration to go the extra mile, for myself this time.

EIGHTEEN
Two More Seconds

After scanning my lungs and blood levels, the hospital released me that same night.

Not a pulmonary embolism. Not a heart attack. Just a severe panic attack – just, as if the word could minimize the way my body had snitched on me in front of everyone I worked with. Just a panic attack that had sent me out of the Palm Beach Courthouse on a gurney, past the stares of my colleagues, my professional reputation trailing behind me like the torn hem of my wedding gown.

Carol drove me home in silence. Sophia was with her father that week – a small mercy. I didn't have to explain the hospital bracelet still circling my wrist, didn't have to pretend I was fine, didn't have to be anyone's mother for a few more days.

The house I had rented was dark when I arrived. I didn't turn on the lights.

The overwhelming feeling of sadness appeared once again, a familiar ache that I'd come to know intimately. A feeling that often steals laughter and dims the light in my eyes.

I'd learned to perfect my make-up, my hair, my smile – a carefully constructed facade that hid the fear in my voice, the hollowness behind my business suit.

The world kept spinning, and I, a ghost in my own life, moved through it, carefully avoiding the reality of the here and now in fear of more disappointment, more abuse, more pain. The more I created my own narrative, even if delusional, the more control I had over my feelings.

But delusion only works until reality kicks down the door.

And reality had just wheeled me out of a courthouse on a stretcher.

That night, alone in the dark, I took inventory.

Fifty years old. Two failed marriages. Three daughters, three different fathers. A body ravaged by stress – the autoimmune disorder spreading like a map of my internal chaos, two pulmonary embolisms survived, a heart that had literally stopped once before. The awards on my desk meant nothing. The international movement I had helped build meant nothing. The 1,300 miles I had walked in a wedding gown meant nothing.

Because I was still injured. My childhood wounds were still raw, hurting, infected.

Twenty-three years since Gladys died. Twenty-three years since I received the vision to walk. And in all that time, I had poured myself into helping other survivors heal while refusing to do the work myself. I had built an empire of service on a foundation of unprocessed trauma.

The foundation had finally cracked.

Sunday night, Sophia was back home with me. After my hospital stay, I was contemplating how the profession I had nearly lost was finally returned to me. I had secured my own place near the beach. I had my dream Jeep. On paper, I was redeemed.

And yet, that night, I felt utterly unworthy – like a fraud who had somehow slipped back into a life she didn't deserve.

I was sitting on the porch, cigarette in one hand, wine in the other. One glass was rare. That night, it was more than one. When I smoke alone, I am usually trying to quiet painful memories. The smoke becomes a ritual of self-punishment, a way to sit with shame. I felt shallow. Empty. Lonely. As if I were rolling in mud I could never wash off. Filth has always been a familiar language to me.

Sophia opened the door and stepped toward me, her small voice cutting through the dark.

"Mommy, how much longer are you going to be outside?"

"Two more minutes, go back inside." I said, sharply.

She stood, immovable, just watching me.

"Didn't I tell you to go inside already?" I watched her sweet eyes drop – not in defiance, but in the shame of feeling rejected. And in that instant, I saw it. I was doing what had been done to me. Not with cords or fists, not with drugs or chaos – but with distance. With irritation. With choosing a cigarette, a drink, and my memories over her.

That night I looked at Sophia, and I saw myself. I saw the little girl who needed reassurance, who felt neglected and never good enough. I already knew I had wounded my older daughters with my volatility and anger. I could not bear the thought of repeating another cycle.

I leaned back in the chair, closed my eyes, and prayed the most dangerous prayer I have ever whispered: "Lord, I am ready to go. I'm tired, my God."

It was not theatrics. It was surrender. And in that surrender, something cracked open. I had spent decades treating symptoms – depression, anxiety, outbursts – while the infected wounds beneath them remained untouched.

That prayer forced me to confront the truth: no job, no degree, no recognition, no relationship would bring me peace. Not even Sophia. Perhaps, not even death.

My answer was buried deeper – beneath achievement, beneath survival, beneath performance. I needed to grieve the child I had been. I needed to accept what happened to her. I needed to stop letting trauma make my decisions.

Shame washed over me for even asking God to take me, as if I were ungrateful for a life that – though imperfect – was precious.

But I also understood something terrifying: I did not know how to live from joy. I only knew how to live from pain and work tirelessly to earn my right to exist. That realization felt heavier than the wine in my veins. As did the insight that hoarding feelings and negative emotions can lead to a toxic internal environment.

I crushed the cigarette, threw the pack away, brushed my teeth, washed my hands, and walked inside. Sophia was waiting. I am usually quick to apologize, to over-explain. That night I didn't have the words. I simply lay beside her and held her.

And for the first time, instead of running from my wounded self, I stayed.

That is where I found myself at the end of 2022.

When we fail to live our truth or accept our reality, we live in a state of delusion where nothing is real, including the decisions that we often think we make. For example, ending a relationship that is harmful. Assessing the gravity of our children's path. Or deciding to abandon everything and everyone, focusing on our emotional healing.

I had been avoiding the decision for over twenty years.

Gladys's death had opened the door for me to examine my trauma. It triggered deep emotions, but I did nothing. I walked 1,300 miles and did nothing. I built a movement and did nothing. I earned degrees and did nothing. I helped thousands of survivors and did nothing – nothing for myself.

Nothing is contraindicated. Nothing can kill you or others. Nothing is dangerous.

The worst thing you can do is nothing. At least when it comes to mental health and trauma.

I was done with nothing.

I contacted Dr. Sobhan and discussed a trauma healing residential program. I voluntarily attended a three-week intensive treatment residential program in Lancaster, Pennsylvania.

The Retreat.

Even the name felt like permission to heal. Permission to stop running. Permission to stop performing. Permission to stop being the advocate, the activist, the movement builder, the mother, the professional – and to just be Josie. Broken, terrified, fifty-year-old Josie, who had never learned how to feel her own feelings without drowning in them.

Sophia stayed with Adrian and Roger. I left my job – another sabbatical, but this time not to rest or contemplate. This time to finally do the hard work that I should have done decades ago.

I was finally going to face my own wounds.

Before I left, Carol sat with me.

Not to talk. Not to advise. Just to sit.

A hand reached out, not to pull me up, but to simply rest beside me in the quiet dark. Carol sat with me, the silence between us rich with unspoken understanding, her presence a soft anchor in the storm. She didn't offer platitudes or easy answers, just the steady rhythm of her breathing, a soft acknowledgment that my pain was real, and I wasn't alone in it.

"You're doing the right thing," she said finally.

I nodded, unable to speak.

The right thing. After all these years. The right thing.

The flight to Pennsylvania was the longest journey I had ever taken – longer than the 1,300 miles in my wedding gown, longer than any road I had walked.

Because this time, I wasn't walking away from me.

I was walking towards my wounded self, having no idea what those open wounds would look like.

NINETEEN
The Retreat

"Self-Love is the balm that soothes the soul."

In January 2023, I was finally ready to abandon everything and everyone, focusing on my emotional healing.

One of the deepest meditations of the entire three-week residential program happened on a night when the temperature had dropped into the twenties and snow was falling quietly outside.

John led the group. He was not a passive facilitator; he was solid, grounded, unapologetically intense. When he worked, he worked with his whole body. He played the guitar, sang, and spoke with a steadiness that felt both safe and unyielding. He did not hide behind clinical distance. He shared pieces of his own trauma, allowing us to see him as human – wounded and healed, broken and rebuilt.

That alone disarmed me.

I remember rushing from the shower, realizing I was late, pulling on my winter boots without socks. By the time I entered the dim room, about twelve of us had already gathered our mats and pillows.

We were a collection of fractured stories trying to find comfort on the floor. I felt strong that night – grounded, present, almost proud of the work I had done. I chose to lie flat on my back. I removed my boots and placed my bare feet on the seat of a chair. The moment my skin touched the cold air, I felt exposed.

My feet have always been sacred territory – untouchable, guarded, off-limits even in romantic relationships. But the lights were already off. John began strumming his guitar. It was too late to retreat.

I shifted slightly, uncomfortable, but didn't want to disrupt the silence. Then I heard his voice float through the dark: "You may feel cold... uncomfortable... unsettled. Stay anyway. Do not run from these uncomfortable moments. Stay. Stay with your pain. Stay with your shame. Stay with your brokenness. Stay with yourself."

The words pierced me. I was already trembling when the melody changed. I couldn't place it at first, just the rhythm of the guitar vibrating through the floor beneath me. And then he sang the first line: "*You've been on my mind...*"

Something hard and cold inside me began to soften. It was as if this young version of me was calling me, asking me to hold her, to trust her, to lead with her instead of against her.

It was not a love song between two people. It was my own inner voice – my younger self and warrior self – begging me for a chance.

I dare you to let me be your one and only. I promise I'm worthy. I was ashamed of that young version of me, but that is the version that kept me alive.

Worthy. That word broke me open. I had built movements, led marches, counseled survivors, stood in front of cameras, testified in rooms of power. But trusting myself? Loving myself? Believing I was worthy to be held by my own arms? That was terrifying.

My bare feet felt like a confession. Emotionally naked. Exposed to the cold. And yet, as the song continued, something warmer than any blanket wrapped around me. The melody became a mantle. Self-acceptance draped over my shoulders. Self-grace poured into places that had only known criticism.

For the first time, I felt tenderness toward myself that did not have to be earned. I wept without restraint. I stayed in the room. I stayed in my body. I stayed with me.

The final night of the program, we had karaoke. None of us were particularly gifted singers – maybe one – but that hardly mattered. We were raw and alive. I sang "Maybe I'm Amazed" for Adrian because we both loved it.

Then I grabbed another woman and insisted we sing "I'm Still Standing." We butchered it. We laughed, cried, hugged, off-key and unpolished, but fully present. It was imperfect and holy at the same time.

The Retreat in Lancaster, Pennsylvania, gave me a kind of healing I had postponed for decades. The tragedy that later followed that program shook me deeply – proof that helping others does not exempt us from tending to our own wounds.

Their story could have been mine: serve, achieve, inspire, and silently unravel. No. Not anymore. Healing before winning is the only strategy that makes sense. We cannot build empires on infected wounds and expect them not to collapse.

Enter the room of your trauma. Stay. Assess the mess. Gather the tools. Clean it – every sore, every disappointment, every lie you told yourself to survive. Sanitize your soul. Do the daily chores of emotional maintenance.

Not for applause. Not for followers. Not for achievement. But so that when the lights go off and the music starts, you can lie there – bare, vulnerable, and finally at peace with yourself.

After that meditation, something in me began to shift. The meditation had opened a door I could no longer pretend wasn't there. During a family therapy session, we contacted my mother in the Dominican Republic. I began asking her the questions I had swallowed for decades – about my stepfather, about the molestation, about the day she sent me away. I needed to know if she understood the intensity of what I had carried. I needed to know if she knew what it cost me.

Except for the rape at nine years old – which she says my grandmother never told her – she remembered everything. Every decision. Every fracture. She told me she was sorry. She told me she was too wounded herself to rescue me.

There was no dramatic collapse. No screaming. Just two women sitting in the aftermath of generations of unhealed pain. For the first time, I saw her as a broken woman who did not know how to save herself. That realization did not erase my wounds – but it loosened their grip.

People ask me, "What did it feel like when you realized you had a breakthrough in your treatment?"

It felt like that night on the floor, barefoot in the cold, when Adele's "One and Only" wrapped around me like a covenant. *I dare you to let me be your one and only. I promise I'm worthy.* The song might be romantic for others but it was redemptive for me. It acknowledged the fear: *I know it ain't easy giving up your heart. Nobody's perfect.* And still it insisted – *give me a chance.*

When the melody met my brokenness and I whispered yes – sobbing, vulnerable, without socks, without makeup, without armor – that was the moment I chose to survive.

I said yes to myself. Yes to loving the woman I had become. Yes to trusting the warrior who had carried me through fire. Yes to the neglected girl who had waited decades for tenderness and acceptance.

That song left me emotionally sore for months. But I noticed the shift. I spoke to myself more kindly. I judged myself less. I would catch my reflection in the mirror and – this may sound silly – I would flirt with myself. Smile. Wink. Admire the strength in my eyes. It was playful and sacred at the same time.

I began creating evenings with myself not out of loneliness, but out of intimacy. I learned to enjoy my own presence.

Do I long for a beautiful partner? Absolutely. I long for someone who can see me, appreciate me, and receive the love I carry. But I no longer rush. I no longer try to force puzzle pieces to fit where they don't belong. I can wait now. Because I am no longer in pain waiting to be rescued by someone to soothe my wounds.

The moment I said yes to that song, yes to that inner voice begging for a chance, I understood something profound: my healing does not live in applause, achievements, or relationships. It lives within me. It walks with me daily. It breathes with me.

I had spent decades working to earn the right to exist. That night, I finally stayed still long enough to truly see the woman I had become. She had survived molestation. Abandonment. Volatility. Shame. Public battles. Private wars. She had built movements. Raised children. Faced herself.

And she was, as I am, beautiful.

Inside and out.

The Retreat helped me heal and taught me how to create a blueprint for my life – taking into consideration my past hurts and considering my current capacity to hold space for myself and for others.

In that controlled environment, I was able to confront, accept, and heal my trauma wounds. For the first time in my life, I wasn't running. I wasn't numbing. I wasn't performing. I was just being – sitting with the pain I had spent decades avoiding.

Upon completion of the residential program, I was enrolled in the Intensive Outpatient Program for ninety days. There, we learned to unpack, repack, and create our own trauma narratives –

befriending our wounds instead of adopting guilt, shame, and resentment for things that we had no control of.

Befriending our wounds.

That phrase changed everything. For so long, I had treated my trauma like an enemy to be defeated. But the Retreat taught me something different: the wounds were part of me. Not all of me – but part of me. And until I stopped fighting them and started listening to them, I would never be whole.

The memories, once twisted and toxic, began to soften and take on a new shape. Each one, a piece of the puzzle that is me. The ownership of it all – not as a burden but as a responsibility, a story I get to shape, mold and transform. And I do it through mindful movement, both physical and emotional.

My healing, like the garden I tend, requires consistent watering and pruning to achieve persistent growth.

I learned to welcome the memories to simply acknowledge their existence – and then gently place them in what I call my "healthy journal." In a plain notebook, the kind you'd find at any store. Sturdy, unremarkable. Inside, the memories sit, stripped of their emotional power, safely contained, their poison neutralized.

My actions, my choices, my future, are determined by the strength of my healthy, present self.

After the Retreat, I understood that healing was as much about the body as it was about the mind.

The sweat stung my eyes, blurring the already hazy dawn. My breath hitched in ragged gasp. My trainer – a UFC champion and sociologist whose childhood past was not much different than mine – simply nodded with gaze steady and encouraging. The subtle pressure of his presence and the intensity of his focus was enough.

Two weeks. Only two weeks into this, and the tears came – hot, uncontrolled rivers down my cheeks. The exertion wasn't to blame. It was a deeper ache, a raw, visceral release that surprised even me.

"It's okay," he murmured, his voice calm. "Your body's releasing. It's all connected."

He explained serotonin, the endorphins, the biochemical ballet of exercise. I knew it all, intellectually, from years spent studying mental health. I could practically recite the textbook chapters on the detrimental effects of nicotine and the inflammatory havoc of poor diet. But knowing and doing were separated by a chasm as wide as the Pacific.

My annoyance was with the mirror reflecting back a person who deliberately sabotaged her own well-being. I was frustrated with me. Each aching muscle, each rasping breath, mirrored the self-inflicted wounds I'd sustained for years.

"Stagnation," he said, the word causing my face to activate like a bad smell had entered the room. He softened it to "sedentary," but the sting remained.

I knew what he meant: the longer we stay paralyzed in a pool of sorrows, painful memories, and regrets, the longer we have to endure in agony the results of our inactions.

He talked about slow, deliberate movements, learning the whispers of my body, its creaks and groans, its surprising reserves of strength. The workouts started gently. Each session was a negotiation, a careful dance between my limitations and his encouragement. Slowly, a grudging flexibility bloomed.

But trauma, he acknowledged, is different. We both knew that no quick fix for the gaping wound of our childhood was available. The loss, he implied, was a permanent fixture – the stolen innocence, the shattered sense of self, remained, a ghost that followed us, a constant, aching reminder of what could never be retrieved.

But we also knew that resilience is not healing – it is simply bouncing back from painful events. Many people are resilient, but very few are brave enough to intentionally embark on a healing journey.

I continue my journey daily, working with my therapist, life coach, and psychiatrist to continue healing, growing, and excelling – for myself, my family, and my community.

I am not co-dependent on these systems in my life; I am interdependent on these systems in my life. I work in community, I heal in community, and I live in community. My doctor, my meds, my pastor, my friends, my co-workers, my neighbors, my grocery store staff, my mall staff – they are all part of my community.

I am not co-dependent on my corner store, but I visit often because they have what I need, and they have created a safe space for me to shop with my family. I could go to another store if I needed to, but for now, this corner store is part of my community.

This was perhaps the most important lesson: healing doesn't happen in isolation. It happens in relationship. It happens in community. It happens when we finally let others see our wounds – and they don't turn away.

In the summer of 2023, I embarked on a cross-country journey with my daughter Sophia – again visiting shelters, sharing Gladys's story, logging miles, and experiencing myself as a single mom on a healing journey.

This time was different from 2001. This time, I wasn't running from my pain. I was walking alongside it.

I placed myself in environments and situations that were new – to experience my growth and newly acquired skills. From Atlanta to Los Angeles, I shared Gladys's story and raised awareness about unresolved trauma, speaking from a place of honesty about my own healing journey that was just beginning.

Sophia and I were accepted into a domestic violence shelter in Alabama – the first shelter we ever entered together. I had prepared us as best as I could. I explained that we would be staying with women and children who were escaping danger, that everyone there had a story, that we needed to be kind and quiet and respectful.

I thought my training, my years of advocacy, my professional language around trauma would somehow buffer the shock.

It didn't. No amount of preparation could have readied us for the atmosphere inside those walls.

The air felt heavy – thick with survival. Children ran through the halls with disorganized, frantic energy, their nervous systems still vibrating from chaos. Their behavior wasn't "bad"; it was untethered. It was trauma searching for ground.

The women moved differently. Some carried visible wounds – arms wrapped in gauze after stabbings, faces marked with bruises trying to fade. Others appeared eerily calm, almost suspended in a trance. They were grateful to be alive, yet hollowed out, unsure of what came next. Safety had arrived, but clarity had not.

That first night, Sophia and I went to bed early. The small room felt both protective and unfamiliar. I could see the questions gathering behind her eyes. *Why does that little boy scream at his mother? Why is that lady's arm wrapped up like that? Why are we here?* It was my job to answer what I could – and to hold what I couldn't.

Before turning off the light, we prayed.

Sophia's prayer was simple, but it carried a depth that humbled me. She prayed for the little boy who would not listen to his mom. She prayed for the woman whose arms were covered in medical bandages after being stabbed. She prayed for the staff who worked so hard to keep everyone safe.

Her words were gentle and specific, as if she were personally introducing each name to God. There was no fear in her voice – only compassion. I remember thinking, *He hears her. Every word.*

When it was my turn, my prayer surprised me.

I did not pray for escape. I did not pray for revenge. I did not even pray for justice. I prayed for life. Long life. Protection. Strength. I prayed to live – not merely survive but live in abundance.

As I held Sophia in my arms that night, something shifted inside me. The woman who had once whispered, "Lord, I am ready to go," now pleaded for more time. More breath. More years. More mornings.

In that shelter, surrounded by the raw aftermath of violence, my desire to live multiplied. I was no longer asking God to take me. I was asking Him to keep me.

And that, too, was healing.

Since my divorce from Adrian, I had remained frozen in fear of going out, dating, and at times, even conceiving that a solid relationship could take place in my life.

That's when I met him – his gaze steady, not flinching from the raw grief I couldn't contain. He didn't try to fix me, just observed my insecurities, my inability to receive what he was offering me.

He showed me I was not ready to date.

I love how Mama had flaunted me. I yearned to be flaunted the way she did. As a single adult looking to be in a relationship, not being hidden is important. I have been in friendships and relationships where I have remained hidden. These types of relationships engulf me in feelings of shame and rejection. I believe – strongly believe – that I was not born to be hidden. I must honor this belief. If I do not, I would be betraying my needs and returning to harmful patterns of behaviors.

I also have learned that when a person walks in light, many of their stains are easily revealed. This realization has allowed me to incorporate every consequence of my maladaptive behaviors, mistakes and every flaw into my healing repertoire. I can't hide my past, nor do I want to. I also don't have to disrobe and show everyone my wounds. But what I do is walk in my truth, daily and unapologetically. I carry my luggage, but I also make use of everything in it. I no longer carry burdens, mine or others, to appear strong. I am strong and smart. I carry what I need and what I use daily and nothing else.

Once I learned to accept my inappropriate behaviors and how these many "flaws" developed, I can practice self-regulation, understand my shadows, and love me regardless of those dark shadows. However, I can't expect everyone to love me and want to flaunt me in the midst of my pain and imperfections. Therefore, I often walk alone.

But Mike – he hadn't just flaunted me; he exploited me: my mind, my body, and even my soul. Finding a person to love me and accept me, my past, and the transformation I had to endure requires a lot, and I don't expect it to be easy.

But I will never settle for someone's company at the expense of being someone I am not. If my daughters, friends, and/or a lover can't appreciate, understand, or honor the woman I had to be and the woman I have become, I prefer to walk away from their presence.

I used to run away from heavy relationships, creating internal chaos and guilt. Now I slowly walk out without shame and with a solid understanding that remaining close to people who can't honor my journey is harmful for my daily recovery. I simply walk away – gently and with self-grace.

That aspect of my healing continues to be the hardest.

In 2024, I began working with men recovering from addiction and trauma – turning pain into purpose. I am currently working in a maximum-security facility, providing therapeutic interventions to men facing charges for violent crimes.

The first time I spoke to a group of incarcerated men about domestic violence and trauma, I expected resistance. What I found was recognition. One after another, men confessed how their own lives had been irrevocably altered by crimes committed against them – a shared trauma that transcended the walls of the prison, connecting us in a way I'd never anticipated.

At the end of my talk, a rough hand clamped down on mine, its grip surprisingly gentle yet firm. The eyes that met mine, though lined with hardship, shone with a gratitude that transcended words. A deep blessing, laced with the wisdom of years spent battling demons, was offered by one of the elders. His prayer followed by a chorus of similar pronouncements. Each one felt like a tangible offering, a warm gift to take with me.

I didn't need to know their names, their stories, their pasts. Their unspoken trust, their quiet vulnerability in sharing their pain, spoke volumes. In that shared moment of human connection, I witnessed the transformative power of grace.

I was so grateful for what the Retreat had given me that a year after my return, I seriously considered going to work for the treatment center that helped me so much.

As I began to apply to the company, I found the sad news.

Several news outlets reported that Peter Schorr, founder and CEO, died by suicide on June 21, 2024. Five days later, Scott Korogodsky, Chief Administrative Officer, also died by suicide. The company had been experiencing financial problems for about a year.

The news devastated me. These were men who had dedicated their lives to helping others heal. And yet.

Our successes, degrees, achievements, or financial status are only parts of us. One part of us does not define us as a whole. I get to choose what defines me – and if I choose work, family, boyfriend, or children, I may find life useless the moment any of these parts that I choose to define me become compromised.

People die by suicide in the midst of divorce, financial crisis, scandals, depressions, misunderstandings, betrayals. Both suicidal and homicidal thoughts are symptoms of mental health crises that must be treated immediately before tragedy happens.

The deaths of Peter and Scott reminded me of what I had learned through my own crisis: we cannot compartmentalize our lives and expect wholeness. We cannot help others heal while refusing to acknowledge our own wounds. We cannot build institutions of healing while neglecting our own hearts.

Surviving trauma is the first step, but healing can be the next messiest experience a person chooses to embark on. It's not a neat, linear process – think more like the "Kingda Ka," once known as the world's tallest and fastest roller coaster in New Jersey. Although my life looked pretty and tidy, just like a roller coaster the up-climb was always accompanied by the fear of the inevitable plummeting drop.

Real or not, this constant survival reaction to life always had me on the defense, trying to justify myself, prove myself, and convince myself that I am, indeed, good enough. Living became exhausting, and at times, unbearable.

Although I did not choose to experience trauma, I learned that I was solely responsible to seek and find my healing. Society often judges, isolates, criticizes, and makes assumptions about trauma survivors. Most people feel untrained and unprepared to assist someone with invisible wounds, even if the survivor is screaming in pain and asking for help.

To choose healing is to choose to show our wounds and become vulnerable.

For those of us scarred by childhood trauma, the path to healing felt like climbing a rocky hill with bare, bleeding hands. Each upward inch a struggle, a desperate search for an edge, a foothold, anything to stop the painful and defeating slide back down. We cling to friends, family – anyone who truly sees us, who gently touches the festering wounds we've been so diligently ignoring.

But I am no longer climbing alone.

The Retreat taught me that. The journey with Sophia reminded me. The men in the maximum-security facility confirmed it. Carol, my therapist, my psychiatrist, my community – they all hold the rope now.

And sometimes, I get to hold it for someone else.

TWENTY
Healing His Bride

Twenty-Five Years Later

For the past twenty-five years, the Brides' March, as we call it in NYC, has continued its annual pilgrimage through Washington Heights, Upper Manhattan, Harlem, and The Bronx – its white tide a constant ebb and flow.

I work hard for every opportunity to attend as often as possible. I have witnessed how the Washington Heights community, their collective heartbeats a steady rhythm, has grieved alongside the Ricart family and the many other families that have lost loved ones. In that shared space, beneath the ever-present chaos of the city, they have continued to heal, purposely, collectively, harmoniously.

In the past twenty-five years, men and women have joined our movement, sharing a common understanding. Some have used their celebrity status or political power to spread the word and elevate our work on a national and international platform.

Our Brides' Walk, no matter the city or country, walks every step with a fierce resolve – a promise to walk the walk, not just speak it.

The Ricart family has never shied away from showing us their grief and their emotional wounds. We walk, we talk, we weep, we hug, we wail and even scream with sorrow – at times – but also with joy.

Their vulnerability has served as a model for the rest of the world to seek the strength they need by exploring their pain in a safe environment amongst people who are emotionally healthier – or at the very least, looking for healing.

Resilience is to continue living and moving forward after a tragedy. But healing is more than moving forward. The power of community healing provides an individual with the ability to restore, educate, and save others by using our truth and our testimonies, in a safe environment and only when we are ready.

Gladys's life became a healing seed.

My soil was barren before I met her. She inspired me to till and turn my memories, pull out weeds from my heart, nourish my soul, water and clean my wounds, to finally protect my landscape.

The journey wasn't a cure. The awareness of my trauma became painful – counseling sessions with my therapist slicing into the deepest wounds and exposing the infected areas. My avoiding behaviors and ineffective coping skills brought on more symptoms, spreading the pain in all areas of my life. I spent decades battling my demons, unwilling to lean in and pay attention to the discomfort that was killing me, literally and fast.

But I must admit that without this awareness, the disease would have been fatal, even if it didn't kill me.

Two decades later, the pain still lingers, but the panic attacks are less frequent, their venom diluted. From time to time, anxiety and depression knock at my door. As a good host, I acknowledge their presence and then politely excuse myself to resume my daily chores.

I don't explain myself. I no longer negotiate with my negative emotions.

I'm in remission – a fragile peace I work to maintain every day. Preventive measures, a healthy lifestyle – these are my daily rituals, my armor against the unexpected phone calls, invitations, and text messages with a seemingly innocent remark, or worse, an emoji.

Healing emotional wounds can be very painful. I continue my journey daily. One sentence, one story, one memory at a time. Understanding that every season of my life can be transformed and wrapped in grace and self-compassion.

Genuine healing, I realized, wasn't about masking imperfections but about embracing them, letting them become stepping stones. It was about the act of tending to the wounded places within, a slow, deliberate process of compassion, understanding, and self-acceptance.

Helping others became a sweeter ritual, a way to pour my own overflowing gratitude onto others – transforming my pain into purpose, my scars into strength.

A single mile? No, the journey stretches onward, towards a horizon ablaze with the light of a million burning bonfires.

We all have an inner voice. It is your job to find yours – to tune in to your wise and beautiful self. To have the strength and character to walk away from whatever it is that does not serve you, respect you, or honor you. But you can't do that if you don't serve, respect, or honor yourself.

For those who share, with gracious reverence, the pain of trauma, let this book be a lifeline. Feel the emotions, smell the scents of your pain as you integrate your memories and begin to discover your past.

Breathe again. Breathe deep and often. Let the dark colors of your memory reemerge, sharp and vibrant. Don't force it – take your time.

Of course it is scary. But it is also worth it to reach your emotional freedom.

The journey of healing is bittersweet.

You will taste the sorrow and feel the despair, but you will also meet the resilience and finally the triumph once you go through the journey.

Take a chance on you. Walk barefoot on your emotional land – feel the weeds, the rocks, the sharp glass from broken dreams. I've been there. I've felt the cold grip of despair, the heavy weight of shame.

But I've also felt the redeeming rain of love and the warm hug of a ray of sunshine. I have finally felt the overwhelming love of myself that allows me to choose joy.

I continue to extend a hand to others, hoping to shorten their journey, to help them build a better life. To create a healthier world, one life at a time, brick by brick. Not reliving the moments but honoring the emotions they unleashed. A plan formed, a slow, steady process of processing, acceptance, and letting go.

I hope you choose to explore, accept, address, and heal your trauma wounds.

May my healing journey bring you the necessary peace and hope to contemplate your own.

Today I chose life.

I am creating my present and helping design the future that I deserve. Intentionally, gracefully, patiently.

Twenty-five years ago, I stood in a wedding gown at the site where Gladys Ricart was murdered. I didn't know then that I was beginning a journey that would change my life – and the lives of countless others.

The wedding gown, once a symbol of Gladys's stolen future, became a symbol of hope. Of resistance. Of healing.

And now, it is a symbol of transformation.

I was eight years old when I first understood that a bride represents family, community, and society.

Now I also understand: Healing a bride is healing civilization.

And to my little Josie…

I see you. I love you. I walk with you every day.

You are safe now, my love.

You did so well keeping us alive.

Te quiero, mi niña.

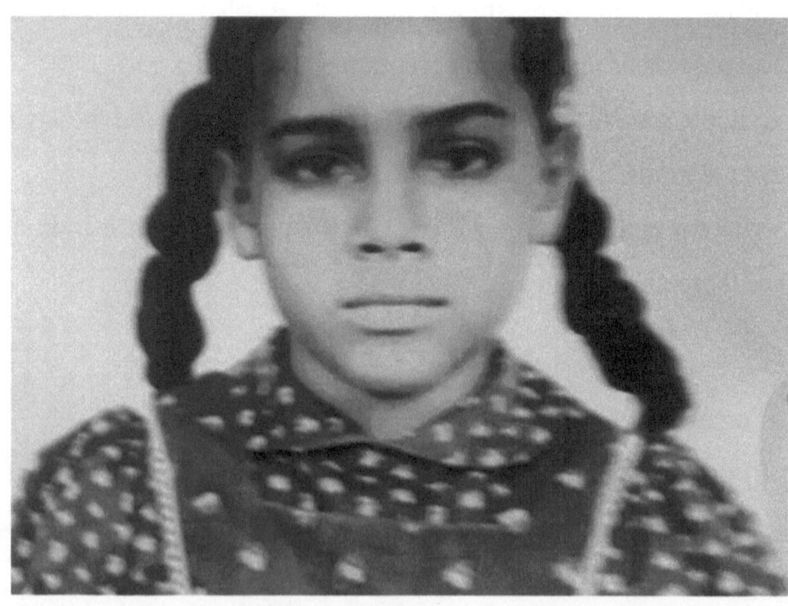

ACKNOWLEDGMENTS

The murder of Gladys Ricart gave life to my activism. Her death awakened something in me that would not rest. What began as grief and outrage slowly transformed into purpose. Through a series of events, that purpose took form in the first Brides' March – a walk from the place where Gladys was murdered to the church where she was meant to be married. What began as a symbolic act of remembrance became a movement that has carried the voices of victims and survivors for more than two decades.

Florida International University and Alpha Phi Sigma made the first steps possible by supporting my vision through a full-time internship under the supervision of Robert Schroder, former Executive Director of the Safespace Foundation. I am deeply grateful to the professors who believed in me when this idea was still fragile and uncertain – Dr. Clinton Terry, Dr. Regina Shearn, and our beloved Dr. Marques. Your encouragement helped turn a student's vision into something much larger than any of us could have imagined.

To Grace Perez – thank you for your patience, your strength, and for seeing the vision from the very beginning. You helped build and sustain this movement for more than twenty years. Your dedication has been one of the quiet pillars behind this work.

John O'Brien, thank you for always honoring, respecting and protecting my mind, body, and soul.

The New York team has remained steadfast, helping the movement grow while continuing to educate, advocate, and develop new strategies to support those who are hurting: Zenaida Mendez, Sally Ramos, Candida Bido, and Milagros Batista de Alianza Dominicana. To the men who stand by us every year and those who lead beside us – Zayid "Baba" Muhammad and Quentin Walcott from Connect NYC – thank you for your leadership and ongoing support. To Erika Miller at Truman High School, for your faithfulness in bringing the most vulnerable population, those high school students who need guidance: the Relationship Abuse Prevention Program has a very special seat at our table. I am especially grateful to my sisters in this work: Maria Lizardo of the Northern Manhattan Improvement Corporation, Margarita Guzman of the Violence Intervention Program, Rosita Romero of the Dominican Women's Development Center, Karina Bernabe, Karina Aybar-Jacobs, Emily Barratta Quinn, Mireya Cruz, Maritza Villacis, and the hundreds of volunteers and survivors who join us every year. Your courage, compassion, and commitment continue to carry this mission forward.

To the many organizations across New York City that walk beside us each year in remembrance, advocacy, and hope – thank you for continuing to stand with us.

I am also grateful to U.S. Congressman Adriano Espaillat, who never left our side – your support has meant more than words can express. To U.S. Congresswoman Gwen Moore, for your confidence in me and for your willingness to embrace this movement without hesitation. To New York State Senator Robert Jackson, thank you for being more than an ally

– thank you for being a friend. And to Assembly Member Amanda Septimo of District 84, thank you for believing in our work and planting seeds that continue to grow.

To the men and women who have allowed me to see into the belly of justice, thank you for the work you do daily to make sure survivors can get a taste of justice: Former Attorney General Robert "Bob" Butterworth, Miami-Dade State Attorney Katherine Fernandez Rundle, and Manhattan District Attorney Alvin Bragg, Jr.

To the Ricart family – especially Yolanda and Juan Ricart – thank you for meeting with me during one of the most painful moments of your lives. Your willingness to share your grief allowed a community of healing to begin to form out of unimaginable loss. Your Sister's life continues to inspire change around the world.

To the Miami team – Laura Finley, Maria Casares-Thorndike, Freddy Frague, Ali Messett, Allison Brimmer, and Bianca Rudge – thank you for standing beside me and believing in this work. I love you all. And to Barry University, thank you for opening your doors, hosting us, and giving this movement a home.

To Moma Doreen, I love you, your tenacity, your wisdom, and your insurmountable amount of grace towards me, my shenanigans, and painful trauma reactions. You are a precious gem and I am blessed to have met you, travel with you, and drink Bahama Mama expecting the headache the next day. Many blessings to you, Moma!

On a personal note, I want to acknowledge my Aunt Doris and my cousin Leo, whom I love like a brother. Thank you for doing your best to protect and guide me.

To my DJJ sisters, Dru Greene and Sandra Johnson, thank you for holding me through every meltdown, helping me early on with the idea of this book and encouraging me to tell this story. And to my unofficial editors and proofreaders – Angela Arias, Jaime Jeffries, Arlene Miller, and Donya Kemp – thank you. You became my strong writing tribe.

To my rescuers – Jennifer Simpson, Joyce Allen, and David Goldizen – thank you for stepping in when I needed it most. Your presence in my life has meant more than I can ever fully express.

To Johanna Neuman, thank you for your guidance and constant support. To Cris Arias from the Miami-Dade State Attorney's Office, thank you for your kindness. Pastor Johnson and Sister Johnson, you have been a blessing. And to Beverly Russell and Carol Brown, Kathleen "Kate" Cole thank you for helping carry me to the finish line. To Mark, thank you for helping me complete the puzzle.

I have been blessed to be surrounded by tribes of extraordinary people who pour into me daily. To the Daniel's Den family, my Glory Call sisters, and my Change Church community – much love.

To the BakeMyBook team, I will always be grateful not only for your services, but for your encouragement, guidance, and for seeing every aspect of my story while helping me shape it with the dignity and respect it deserves. Thank you for reminding me that my story is worthy of love, care, and kindness – even during its most unflattering moments.

Theo, thank you for holding my hand through this process with such love and grace. To you, your wife, your amazing team, and my dear Francesca, I will always be grateful.

And finally, to every survivor who has trusted me enough to place your pain in my hands to hold – thank you for the honor.

We are enough.

Photo by Myiah Brown

ABOUT THE AUTHOR

I was born in the Dominican Republic and raised in the chaos of survival. I became an advocate, an activist, a counselor, and finally, a woman brave enough to heal herself.

I hold a Master's in Clinical Mental Health Counseling and have spent thirty years serving survivors of domestic violence, sexual assault, and trauma. I am the founder of The Brides' March and a proud mother of three daughters.

Today, I choose life. I live in South Florida, where I continue to walk... one step, one story, one breath at a time.

Read more on www.josieashton.com and www.bridesmarch.com

Reflections